DEDICATION

This book is dedicated to my seven grandchildren: Tommy Nolan, Natalie Nolan, Michael Nolan, Lauren Clark, Drew Clark, Claire Clark and Annabelle Clark.

I'm so proud of each of you, and the unique individuals you are. I claim for you the sure promises of God:

"All thy children shall be taught of the Lord;
and great shall be the peace of thy children."
– Isaiah 54:13

"For I will contend with the one who contends
with you, and I will save your sons."
– Isaiah 49:25

"Your descendants will possess nations, and
they will resettle the desolate cities."
– Isaiah 54:3

"Sons in their youth...like well-nurtured plants, and
our daughters...like pillars carved to adorn a palace."
– Psalm 144:12

CONTENTS

CHAPTER 1   I WISH I HAD KNOWN   7

CHAPTER 2   SELF, SUBMISSION AND SEX   17

CHAPTER 3   THE SONS AND MOTHERS OF ISRAEL   33

CHAPTER 4   TEN WOMEN WORTH EMULATING   67

CHAPTER 5   SILENT NO MORE!   96

CHAPTER 6   YOUR SPECIAL GIFT   107

CHAPTER 7   TIME FOR A CHANGE   121

CHAPTER 1

$\mathcal{I}$ WISH I HAD KNOWN

$\mathcal{I}$ f you have read my book, LIFE IN THE RIGHT SEAT, you know that I was born into a family with an alcoholic, abusive father who my mother left about the time I entered high school.

For my entire childhood, our family moved often because my dad, a heavy equipment operator, traveled from one job site to another. As a result, I had little social or community life, and any new friends were soon left behind as we pulled up stakes and headed for the next town.

Both of my parents had come from disconnected families themselves and had little concept of how to build—let alone maintain—a healthy home life. There was practically no family structure in which to take comfort.

Spiritually, for as long as I can remember, I yearned to know more about God. As a four year old, I was taken to a revival meeting at a Nazarene church where I responded to the altar call and gave my heart to the Lord Jesus. Sadly, there was rarely anyone, or anything to nurture my young faith.

My sister and I would often attend the nearest church, regardless of the denomination, but no one accompanied us. Yet the Lord was faithfully watching over me.

A HANDSOME YOUNG AIRMAN

During my high school years, my mother remarried. Her new husband was in the military, and we moved to the San Francisco Bay area. Being new, I wasn't sure how to fit into the social scene. But Hamilton Air Force Base had a nice swimming pool, and military families were free to enjoy it. Thus at the age of 16, I met a handsome young airman named Garth Coonce who was stationed there.

Although he was four years older, one year later we were married in a small ceremony at the chapel on the military base. Neither of us were living for the Lord at the time.

"I WISH"

To say I was ready for marriage is laughable. I had no clue what to expect and virtually no preparation for what was ahead. With her limited background, my mother raised me the best she could.

Looking back, much was lacking in my knowledge

and experience:

- I wish I had known what was expected of a wife.
- I wish I had known God's pattern for order and authority in the home.
- I wish I had known the place of submission in a healthy marriage.
- I wish I had known that God's Word contains the principles by which to build a healthy home.
- I wish I had known the "gifts" the Lord had placed within me.

All of this came later, as the direct result of a commitment I made to surrender my total life to God. As I began to delve into His Word, the Lord literally transformed my life—and our marriage.

If, when I was a teen, you would have told me, "Tina, some day you will be ministering with your husband to millions around the world through television," I would have thought you were out of your mind!

This is why I am willing to share the personal things in this book with you. Regardless of your upbringing, if you are open to His calling, the Lord can make you the person He has destined you to be.

A Twisted Understanding

Countless women, including myself, had fathers who

were not godly men. Others may have a boyfriend and eventually a husband who has a skewed view regarding spiritual matters.

You may have experienced this yourself. As a result, it can be difficult for women with such a background to truly understand the love which is extended by your Heavenly Father. If there is nothing on earth by which to make a comparison, how can we comprehend what the Lord offers?

Because of inadequate role models, many women are twisted in their understanding of love—one which provides, protects, nurtures, teaches, and is always faithful and near at hand. We see real love in the Lord's promise: *"I will not fail you nor forsake you"* (Joshua 1:5).

GROWING IN GRACE

The father-daughter relationship is extremely important since such interaction—or lack of it—affects her view of life. If the father is absent, abusive or not fulfilling his proper role, it makes it extremely difficult for her to fully understand the concept of a caring Heavenly Father. She can become resentful and bitter, subconsciously thinking, "If my own father was a jerk, and I couldn't depend on him, why should I trust God?" Or she can seek love in the arms of other men, vulnerable to exploitation.

Again and again, as I grew in grace, I asked the Holy Spirit to open my eyes and show me how to accept my

Father's role in my life—and He did.

Little by little you learn through God's Word that you can trust the Lord. He will never harm, abandon or embarrass you. He cares about your dignity and wants you to be happy and live a peaceful life.

The Bible tells us the King's daughters are beautiful, inside and out (Psalm 45). They are a fulfillment of the joy and grace He works within you. In fact, the Lord delights in causing you to become a radiant and secure person with the glow of His presence.

"WIRED" DIFFERENTLY

As a newlywed, I had the notion Garth and I would automatically "think alike" on every topic and never have a cross word. Wow, was I wrong!

It didn't take long for me to realize that men and women are totally different, no matter how much affection they have for one another.

God "wired" us uniquely.

For example, we often laugh and joke about the male ego, but the fact is, that is how the creator made them. Even though they may appear very macho, men are extremely sensitive to criticism—probably more so than women.

A major difference between men and woman is that men are usually reluctant to reveal their emotions because it is uncomfortable for them. Women usually don't have a problem letting others know how they feel.

A man, however, when stung by words or actions, will be deeply wounded—but the issue will crop up much later, when the reaction is least expected.

It takes patience, practice and prayer for a woman to learn how to express her feelings to a man who may have caused a problem through his own insensitivity. She needs to master the fine art of addressing problems without damaging his ego, and still express her confidence in him. She will artfully sandwich a small amount of correction between two thick slices of praise!

"THEN WHAT?"

Even though men and women may be polar opposites in their abilities and calling, God can use both to fulfill His purpose.

There was a time when I used to lead people in praise and worship with my guitar in numerous groups and churches. I knew it was an anointing for that ministry, not from great musical ability or voice. Often I would lead others into the lovely presence of God through praise and worship, but then I wasn't sure what to do from there.

That's where Garth's abilities came to the surface. He knew exactly how to take over the service and minister to the people. You see, the Lord used each of us in separate ways—yet together we were accomplishing His will.

WHO'S IN CHARGE?

In the early days of our television ministry, I worked along side of Garth and we both put in countless hours every week. Yet our styles were very different.

Without question, he was the decision maker, but I was often tempted to say, "Well, since I am investing the same amount of time as you, don't you think I am entitled to have a say in what happens around here?"

After all, I figured I had an equal slice of experience and being so close to the situation, I knew a few things he didn't. But Garth would have the final word and say, "This is the way it's going to be."

As a woman, I had learned enough about God's laws of leadership to know my role was not to push, control or manipulate.

I learned to realize that ultimately God is in charge. And often in life, many of the things we fight for so valiantly, are minor issues compared to the big picture. Only what the Lord says really matters.

Years ago, when I was complaining about a certain issue, our daughter, Vicki Clark, summed it up brilliantly. She said, "Mom, what it boils down to is that you and Dad have different styles of leadership. You think your way is better—and it may be—but that doesn't mean his won't work."

Her astute observation really shut my mouth!

Over time I realized what was happening in the ministry of TCT was far greater than any one man or woman. Thankfully, Garth has a genuine heart that seeks to please God and a wise, balanced approach to administration. There has never been a temptation of any kind for him to glorify himself in any way—to be honest, he doesn't even enjoy being on television. Rather, Garth simply tackles whatever the Lord says needs to be done, setting the standard he expects the team members to follow.

X, Y and Z

In business, people often speak of X and Y styles of management. This theory came from Doug McGreggor, a social psychologist, in his book, THE HUMAN SIDE OF ENTERPRISE.

The X style is extremely masculine—an authoritarian, "my way or the highway" approach. The Y style is a softer, kinder, "team building" method of management.

Then someone proposed a Z style of leadership, combining the best features of the two.

The point being, two different approaches do exist—not just in business, but also in marriage.

The Mission

There were times when I thought Garth was absolutely dead wrong about an issue—particularly in dealing with individuals. The mother's heart in me wants to be kind to everybody and have one big happy family.

I never like to see anyone in trouble or terminated from employment.

As a leader, however, he has a responsibility to look at the overall mission, not individuals. He is a trustee of the vision—regardless of what someone's feelings may be at the moment.

Of course he wants to be kind and gracious to people—that goes along with being a Christian gentleman, a representative of the Father. But sometimes there are decisions, however painful, which must be made.

DIFFERENT PATHS

I have to admit, it was a difficult day for me when the ministry grew to the point Garth said, "Tina, I don't think we need to be in the office every day. If we fail to start delegating the daily affairs of our work, the ministry won't be able to grow."

As the leader, he tried to explain to me, "We will be bogged down in the daily grind forever and limit the number of people we can touch with the Gospel."

I struggled with his decision because I was actually happy and secure being there, yet I knew he had been praying over the matter and was absolutely right.

Through these experiences I have come to the conclusion that men and women are usually reaching for the same goal, yet traveling on separate paths and using different methods. So, as a woman and partner, I have learned to allow him to pursue his plans with my help—not my interference.

LOVE VS. RESPECT

We usually link the words "love" and "respect" together. But in both marriage and ministry, I've learned there is a difference between them.

It can baffle women how most men will *respect* another man, and overlook his faults. They may not *love* such an individual, or even like him, but they can *respect* him because of some ability.

Yet God requires a man to *love* his wife—and, because of his nature, it is often difficult for him to demonstrate his love.

At the same time, the Lord requires a wife to *respect* her husband. While it is her nature to shower him with *love*, often she does not know how to show *respect*.

In the next chapter we will look at ways these two needs can be met.

CHAPTER 2

SELF, SUBMISSION AND SEX

*D*uring the years when Garth was in the corporate world, I wrestled with the fact that he was more concerned with his career than helping around the home. Yet I realized God had given him unique abilities and callings that did not include housework and child care. I had to learn there is a principle of biblical submission.

Garth is at his best in toe-to-toe, hardball business activities. He's an absolute master in this arena. That's something I know nothing about. If our livelihood depended on me doing it, we would starve to death in a week! But I'm proud to be one heck of a housekeeper!

How foolish it would be for me to get upset with him because he left wet towels on the bathroom floor or didn't make the bed! Yet, we are total partners in life and marriage.

Be "Subject"?

The issue always reverts back to the word *self.* Are you going to live God's way or yours? Are you willing to yield to your spouse and give deference to one another—and be more willing for your partner to have the preeminence than you?

That principle actually applies everywhere we go in life, whether it is in the workplace or at home.

We can't ignore or get away from the strong teaching in God's Word regarding the topic of submission. For marriage it is clear: *"Wives, be subject to your husbands, as is fitting in the Lord. Husbands, love your wives and do not be embittered against them"* (Colossians 3:18-19).

As Christ Loved the Church

There is something noble about a woman who follows the biblical pattern and pleases her husband in a righteous, dignified way—not with any hidden motives or agenda or simply "putting on an act."

The example, of course, is Christ and the church. *"Wives, be subject to your own husbands, as to the Lord. For the husband is the head of the wife, as Christ also is the head of the church, He Himself being the Savior of the body. But as the church is subject to Christ, so also the wives ought to be to their husbands in everything. Husbands, love your wives, just as Christ also loved the church and gave Himself up for her"* (Ephesians 5:22-25).

That's a pretty tall order!

An Honest Heart

How do you submit to the Lord? Sometimes women make the mistake of feeling holy and righteous over their husband, sending the unspoken message, "I'm serving God and you're not."

Not only will such an attitude turn a guy off, it shuts out the grace and presence of the Holy Spirit to work in and through him.

The way you submit yourself to your own husband as you would to the Lord is with a true, honest heart, trying to serve and please—in a way that is meaningful to him.

But remember, the husbands have their own instructions. They are to love their wives as Christ loved the church—meaning He was totally committed to her welfare no matter what it cost Him—even His life.

Paul concludes this passage by saying, *"Nevertheless, each individual among you also is to love his own wife even as himself, and the wife must see to it that she respects her husband"* (Ephesians 5:33).

Here is how this verse reads in the Amplified Bible: (Take time to read it carefully. It explains it well!) *"However, let each man of you* [without exception] *love his wife as* [being in a sense] *his very own self; and let*

the wife see that she respects and reverences her
husband [that she notices him, regards him, honors him,
prefers him, venerates, and esteems him; and that she
defers to him, praises him, and loves and admires him
exceedingly].

WHAT WE REQUIRE

Why does the Bible say a man should "love" his wife,
but a woman should "respect" her husband?

It is because the God who created us knows our needs
and makeup. Women require love and affection while
men require respect and honor—very different things.

A man's need for respect doesn't mean he is some
sort of ego maniac. It is a legitimate need—a picture of
how God wants and deserves our respect regarding who
He is.

Many women don't realize they are to admire their
husband, giving him honor and dignity, both in the home
and out. Instead, they sometimes get together and start
"dissing" their spouses. One starts, then the next jumps
in, "Well, mine is worse than yours." Before long it
becomes an unpleasant display of criticism and
complaint.

We are to behave, *"With all humility and gentleness,
with patience, showing tolerance for one another in love,
being diligent to preserve the unity of the Spirit in the
bond of peace"* (Ephesians 4:2-3).

Seeing the Good

The man who loved and cared enough to ask you to spend your life with him, has the right to that esteem—even if he sits in front of the television with a beer can in his hand!

You may say, "But Tina, you don't know what a louse he is. When I married him, I didn't know what he was really like."

Well, the Bible has an answer for that in Philippians 4:8: *"Finally, brethren, whatever is true, whatever is honorable, whatever is right, whatever is pure, whatever is lovely, whatever is of good repute, if there is any excellence and if anything worthy of praise, dwell on these things."*

If there has ever been anything worthy your husband has done, that's what to think about and focus on. Discipline your mind and bring every thought into subjection (1 Corinthians 10:5).

I could think of many things Garth has done over the years that I didn't like. I could dwell on them, turning them over and over in my mind, until I get mad all over again—and then wonder why I'm miserable!

But God's Word tells me to do exactly the opposite. I can think of the countless things he has done right, and recognize the efforts he has put forth. I am to see him through the Lord's eyes—and remember the commendable things my husband has accomplished.

Fixing my mind on the positive rather than the negative brings peace. It also allows the Holy Spirit to work. He won't linger around where there is anger, strife and contention. And after all, isn't that what we want others to do for us? To appreciate our good intentions and actions, overlook our faults, and give us the benefit of the doubt when there is a question.

When you begin to practice this divine principle, you will start to see a welcome difference in your marriage. If you treat your husband like a king, you could be surprised at how soon he starts acting like one. You'll see your husband respond to you in a loving, tender, kind and understanding way.

THE PATH TO FULFILLMENT

Paul tells us to, *"Be devoted to one another in brotherly love; give preference to one another in honor"* (Romans 2:10).

What a beautiful phrase.

Sadly, in the body of Christ we often see exactly the opposite taking place: contentions, jealousy, manipulations, trying to get ahead, making oneself look important instead of building up and edifying others.

"Giving preference" and putting other's needs first (regardless of ours) is the genuine way to happiness and fulfillment. When we sincerely consider others more important than ourselves, believe me, the Lord knows how to exalt us when the time is right.

"THAT'S NOT FAIR!"

But being in submission doesn't mean you are a doormat having no voice or choice. We do not live in the world of the Taliban!

As a Christian woman, support and help your husband in whatever he does. With God's help, this is what I have done. And I've learned His way is always the right way!

Some still insist, "That's not fair. A woman should be equal, just as important as a man."

In the eyes of God we are, yet for anything to run smoothly somebody has to be in charge; there must be an order of things. Without that, there is chaos.

Can you imagine an Army going to war without a general devising an overall strategy, giving orders, and soldiers obeying the plan?

When self-interest dictates action, you have a situation written about in the Bible, where *"every man did what was right in his own eyes"* (Judges 17:6). The result is total confusion.

As a newlywed, Garth would tell me, "Anything that has two heads is a monster!"

I had no idea what he was talking about. He would accuse me of trying to manipulate him or control things—and I didn't have a clue. I really didn't know I was upsetting him. I just felt I knew a few things and once in a while he ought to listen to me.

I didn't realize his perception was that I was trying to

be the "head," and override his authority.

An "Imperishable Quality"

During the early years of our marriage, when I was becoming deeply involved in spiritual matters and Garth was still living in the world, I carefully read what Peter said concerning the matter of submission. He was speaking to women who had unsaved husbands.

Peter writes, *"...wives, be submissive to your own husbands so that even if any of them are disobedient to the word, they may be won without a word by the behavior of their wives, as they observe your chaste and respectful behavior. Your adornment must not be merely external—braiding the hair, and wearing gold jewelry, or putting on dresses; but let it be the hidden person of the heart, with the imperishable quality of a gentle and quiet spirit, which is precious in the sight of God. For in this way in former times the holy women also, who hoped in God, used to adorn themselves, being submissive to their own husbands; just as Sarah obeyed Abraham, calling him lord, and you have become her children if you do what is right without being frightened by any fear. You husbands in the same way, live with your wives in an understanding way, as with someone weaker, since she is a woman; and show her honor as a fellow heir of the grace of life, so that your prayers will not be hindered"* (1 Peter 3:1-7).

You may say, "This doesn't apply to me," or "You

don't know my circumstances." Yet, we cannot deny or ignore the principles of submission in God's Word.

The first verse in the above passage tells wives to "*be submissive to your own husbands*"—not to anyone else's husband, or to all men in general!

"WITHOUT A WORD"

The strongest testimony you will ever have is the silent conduct of your life—living in reverence and obedience to the Lord, and to your husband if you are married.

To live in submission does not mean to be browbeaten or abused.

The admonition of Peter regarding winning your husband to the Lord is to keep your mouth shut—"*without a word.*" Let your actions do the talking!

We are also told not to be overly concerned with outward appearance. Though of course we should do the best we can with whatever we have to work with—it's what's on the inside that really counts.

WASHING FEET

In the Kingdom of God, things work differently than they do in the world. In the Lord's view, the way up is down! If Jesus was willing to wash the feet of His disciples, why shouldn't we?

The Son of God says a servant is not above his master (Matthew 10:24) and we should be willing to follow His example and be open to graciously meeting the needs of others.

THE LORD COMES FIRST

There are several verses in the Bible which are "foundational" to my life.

- *"Trust in the Lord with all thine heart; and lean not unto thine own understanding. In all thy ways acknowledge him, and he shall direct thy paths"* (Proverbs 3:5-6 KJV).
- *"I have learned to be content in whatever circumstances I am"* (Philippians 4:11).
- *"Whatever your hand finds to do, do it with all your might"* (Ecclesiastes 9:10).
- *"Whatever you do in word or deed, do all in the name of the Lord Jesus"* (Colossians 3:17).
- *"...present your bodies a living sacrifice, holy, acceptable unto God, which is your reasonable service"* (Romans 12:1 KJV).

In case you didn't notice, there is one central theme—placing God first and serving Him with our whole heart.

The Question of Divorce

When two people come together and make a vow "for better or for worse" it is made in total faith and belief they are going to live happily ever after.

Once the honeymoon is over, however, because of the daily grind of living, the qualities you originally saw in your spouse can begin to show imperfections. Before long, their once-cute habits become annoying and aggravating. Opposites may attract, but after awhile they attack! And there are conflicts of opinion regarding how things are to be done.

Eventually, one frustrated partner says, "I just can't handle this. I don't want to live with you anymore." They walk away, forsaking their vows and pursuing their own life.

But for the married woman who has made a commitment both to her husband and to Christ, leaving is not an option. Although the Bible certainly makes room for dissolving a union when there are extreme circumstances —physical cruelty or infidelity.

The Unbelieving Spouse

The apostle Paul wrote to the believers at Corinth, *"...to the married I give instructions, not I, but the Lord, that the wife should not leave her husband (but if she does leave, she must remain unmarried, or else be reconciled to her husband), and that the husband should not divorce his wife"* (1 Corinthians 7:10-11).

This can be interpreted as allowing a time of separation to cool things off before trying a new start.

I've heard women say, "My husband and I aren't compatible. I love the things of God and he doesn't."

Well, according to scripture this is no reason for divorce. In the same chapter, Paul speaks to both husbands and wives on this very issue: *"...if any brother has a wife who is an unbeliever, and she consents to live with him, he must not divorce her. And a woman who has an unbelieving husband, and he consents to live with her, she must not send her husband away. For the unbelieving husband is sanctified through his wife, and the unbelieving wife is sanctified through her believing husband; for otherwise your children are unclean, but now they are holy"* (vv.12-14).

In the spiritual realm there is somehow a covering for the unsaved spouse until the time this person becomes a believer.

BEHIND CLOSED DOORS

If a wife truly pleases her husband, he will do anything in his power for her—just as Jesus will for His bride. Whatever she asks, He will do.

Let me bring this closer to home.

One of the most common problems in marriage is a sexual one. Why? Because in the natural order of things most men desire sex much more than women. Physiologically, he has a a greater need in this area.

The most godly young couple, raised in the church all their lives can be united in marriage and it's not long before the husband may be praying, "Lord, I love my wife and thank You for her, but why did You have to give me an iceberg?"

At the same time, she may be praying, "God, thank You for giving me a wonderful man, but why did You have to give me a sex maniac?"

THE ISSUE OF INTIMACY

Sometimes the roles are reversed! But whatever the case, the Bible tells us that in marriage, you give yourself to your partner and become one flesh (Genesis 2:24). Your body is not your own. *"The wife does not have authority over her own body, but the husband does; and likewise also the husband does not have authority over his own body, but the wife does"* (1 Corinthians 7:4).

Ask the Lord to give you a willing heart to meet the needs of your spouse. If you loathe sex and use every excuse to avoid physical intimacy, it is time to seek God for help. Perhaps find a qualified counselor and talk honestly with your spouse about your feelings.

Sexual intimacy is ordained by God and is considered acceptable behavior by Him.

It all comes down to yielding to the Lord and being willing to give up self, whatever the situation.

For women, the marriage bed is a place to build your husband up, and make him feel good about himself. It has been said this way, "A wise woman will be a lady in public, a mother and hostess at home, and a tiger in the bedroom!"

Where the Anointing Begins

The Bible says we can't come to Christ unless the Holy Spirit draws us. And it's usually the same way in a marriage. The husband desires a relationship and communion with his wife physically, and she is to respond.

But if she refuses because of "feeling hurt" she is denying him what he needs.

The Bible tells us the marriage relationship is like the relationship between Christ and His bride, the church. When the church truly worships, giving Him the honor He deserves, He responds by pouring out a precious anointing of the Holy Spirit that heals, strengthens, and changes things.

In the same way, when personal intimacy in marriage is right, an anointing will flow forth bringing healing throughout your home and life.

Put Fun in Your Marriage

Beside loving your husband as he needs to be loved and admired, ask yourself this question: "Am I fun to live with?"

To put a spark into your marriage, let me encourage

you to think of silly things to do to make him anxious and excited to come home. Write humorous notes. Dim the lights and burn some candles! Let laughter be heard.

Ask God to give you wisdom to make him feel special—esteemed and honored. Remember, however, not every husband is the same. What turns one guy on will be a turn-off to another.

When I first began to learn these simple but effective techniques, I would take a lipstick and write a love note to Garth on the bathroom mirror. He couldn't miss it!

THE BACK RUB!

There was a period when Garth was not living for the Lord, though I was active in numerous ministries, including church at least three times a week. But the Lord began to give me wisdom in some of these areas. I was careful to avoid making him feel neglected or threatened by my outside interests.

Often I'd arrive home from prayer meeting and find Garth laying on the floor watching TV—usually something I felt was most "unspiritual."

Instead of being critical, I would get down on the floor and begin to rub his back and shoulders. All the time, I was silently praying in the Spirit, yet giving him my full attention, and he loved it.

During the commercials I would chat with him concerning things going on at church, and ask his opinion about them—honoring him by regarding his insight as valuable. And it was!

Even though he wasn't yet surrendered to the Lord, a male's natural no-nonsense logic can cut through a lot of cloudiness. And you know what? Before long he was attending church with me.

DISCIPLINE YOUR EMOTIONS

The Bible says, *"The heart of her husband doth safely trust in her, so that he shall have no need of spoil. She will do him good...all the days of her life"* (Proverbs 31:11-12 KJV).

This means if a wife fulfills the role God intends, making a secure and happy home, her husband is not going to stray into activities he shouldn't.

Giving yourself to your husband is being obedient to God's Word. But it must come from a willing heart, not a resentful one. To rewrite 1 Corinthians 13:3: *"Even though I give my body to my husband, resenting it, gritting my teeth until it is over, it profits me nothing."*

We need to be honest before the Lord, asking Him to help us become the wife He wants us to be. Sometimes that requires disciplining our thoughts, emotions, and mouth in order to please our spouse. Your husband deserves this, just as the Lord is honored and obeyed by His bride, the church.

CHAPTER 3

*T*HE SONS AND MOTHERS OF ISRAEL

*W*hat a rich heritage we have!

When we look back to our spiritual lineage we learn that Abraham was chosen by God to be *"...the father of a multitude of nations"* (Genesis 17:5).

The Almighty promised, *"I will make you exceedingly fruitful, and I will make nations of you, and kings will come forth from you. I will establish My covenant between Me and you and your descendants after you throughout their generations for an everlasting covenant, to be God to you and to your descendants after you"* (vv.6-7).

But don't forget, the Lord's promise also included Abraham's wife, Sarah. God declared, *"I will bless her, and indeed I will give you a son by her. Then I will bless her, and she shall be a mother of nations; kings of peoples will come from her"* (v.16).

It happened! Even though the "father and mother of nations" were well past their child-bearing years, God gave them a son named Isaac—and in turn Isaac and his wife Rebekah bore a son named Jacob.

Following years of turmoil, Jacob (whose name is usually translated "deceiver" or "supplanter"), spent a night in prayer where the angel of the Lord actually wrestled with him. It is a fascinating drama of spiritual truth!

After many hours, with one touch, the angel deliberately threw Jacob's hip out of joint, thus disabling him. At that point, all Jacob could do was hang onto the conqueror with all his might—clinging to the one stronger than himself. Finally, the angel exclaimed, *"Let me go, for the dawn is breaking"* (Genesis 32:26). He was saying, "The time has come to go on to a new phase of your life."

Jacob now knows he is utterly dependent on his victor and, with fierce determination, replied, *"I will not let you go until you bless me"* (v.26).

The angel then asked, *"'What is your name?'"* —forcing him to admit his character and face himself.

He replied, "Jacob."

Then the angel declared, *"Your name shall no longer be Jacob, but Israel; for you have striven with God and with men and have prevailed"* (v.28).

This new name was indicative of a new nature, with the spiritual capacity for being a blessing to mankind. From that moment forward, Jacob "the deceiver" and "heel grabber" became Israel, a prince of God and "overcomer."

A Spiritual Progression

Modern Israel stills bears the name change given by God to Jacob. His offspring were not called "The twelve sons of Jacob," rather "The twelve sons of Israel."

As I began to study the lives of these men, I saw a parallel in their birth order to the spiritual progression you and I travel as believers. I also became aware that even though these were to become men who would lead the twelve tribes of Israel, the meaning of their names were related to what their *mothers* were experiencing at the time. The role of the woman was evident in shaping their personalities and eventual destinies.

Development and progression are essential to the Christian life. As one believer said, "I thank God I am not what I used to be, but I'm not what I am going to be."

We are all in a constant state of growth and development.

Let's examine the lives of these twelve sons:

Son Number One:
Reuben

As was common in Old Testament times, Jacob had two wives, Rachel and Leah. To complicate the matters, they were sisters!

Rachel was the pretty one who was dearly loved by Jacob, while Leah was who we would refer to as the "ugly duckling" and was *tolerated* rather than greatly appreciated.

The Bible gives this description: *"And Leah's eyes were weak, but Rachel was beautiful of form and face"* Genesis 29:17).

Many of us can identify with Leah's plight—feeling unattractive and unloved.

In those days, a woman's worth was measured by how many children she could give to her husband, and it must have come as quite a surprise when *"...the Lord saw that Leah was unloved, and he opened her womb, but Rachel was barren"* (v.31).

Into the world was born a son and she named him Reuben, which stands for, "See, a son." In other words, Leah was triumphantly announcing, "See, God gave me a son first!"

From the very beginning, you and I can begin to identify with the sons of Israel. At the moment when we are born again and become the sons and daughters of the Living God, all of heaven can say about us, "See, a son." We are born of Christ—little "Ruebens" running around God's earth!

THE HEAVENLY BRIDEGROOM

Leah said of her son's birth, *"Because the Lord has seen my affliction; surely now my husband will love me"* (v.32). She was right. God did see her—He sees everything!

When you and I are mired in anguish, feeling unappreciated, the Lord is still watching over us. Even when the children of Israel were suffering in their slavery under Pharaoh, *"God heard their groaning; and God remembered His covenant with Abraham, Isaac, and Jacob. God saw the sons of Israel, and God took notice of them"* (Exodus 2:24-25).

At this point, poor Leah didn't know anything of the love of God, or that in the years to come the Lord would reveal himself as the heavenly bridegroom, the husband who is forever married to the backslider. In Isaiah, the prophet would elaborate on this, saying, *"...your husband is your Maker, whose name is the Lord of hosts"* (Isaiah 54:5).

Often, because of family background, some women do not have a good image of a husband since they have not seen a proper role model. They need to know their Heavenly Bridegroom will care for them.

Remember, we are Ruebens and have just come into the family of God. We don't know the depths, riches, goodness or the love of our Father. But, hopefully, we are ready to learn.

THE RESPONSIBILITY FACTOR

As Reuben matured, he was like most of us, a mixture of personality traits. Being the firstborn son of Jacob, he had the rights of the inheritance—a double blessing and a double portion. He also had the obligation of walking in his father's footsteps, to carry his spiritual birthing as well as a spiritual *responsibility*. And he made a half-hearted attempt to fulfill his calling—as some of us do.

However, we do observe some good qualities in Reuben, especially the fact he wasn't cruel and crafty like some of his brothers.

I'm sure you remember the story of Joseph's brothers being so jealous of him they wanted to take his life. It was Reuben who spoke up and said, *"'Shed no blood. Throw him into this pit that is in the wilderness, but do not lay hands on him'— that he might rescue him out of their hands, to restore him to his father"* (Genesis 37:22).

Apparently Reuben was absent when the caravan of spice traders passed by and Joseph's brothers pulled him from the pit and sold him as a slave into Egypt for twenty pieces of silver.

Reuben knew as the firstborn he would have to bear the responsibility for what happened to Joseph.

He Was Accountable

Years later, as his brothers were standing before Joseph in Egypt, talking among themselves and not realizing he was the governor, it was Reuben who reminded them what they did to their brother years earlier. He never forgot his responsibility.

When Joseph, whose identity still hadn't been

revealed, asked, "Do you have a younger brother?" they answered honestly. Joseph, wanting to see his brother Benjamin again, demanded, "Don't return for more food unless you bring him with you."

Back in Canaan, Rueben was the one who told hesitant Jacob, *"You may put my two sons to death if I do not bring him back to you; put him in my care and I will return him to you"* (Genesis 42:37).

FAILING THE TEST

One of the most serious mistakes Reuben ever made was to yield to sexual immorality—and it cost him his rights and position of leadership.

This is a topic we don't like to talk about in the body of Christ today, but "Reubens," who are blood-washed children of God, are tempted in sexual ways.

Reuben failed his test and slept with Bilhah, the handmaid of his step-mother, Rachel (Genesis 35:22).

Perhaps subconsciously, Rueben was trying to avenge the treatment Jacob gave to his own mother, Leah—that he didn't treat her kindly.

You and I can lose the potential God has for us if we have a lack of self-discipline and respect for authority—whether earthly or spiritually. Reuben was shortsighted like Saul, who also lost his position of leadership in the same way.

Before the patriarch Jacob died, he pronounced blessings and cursings upon his sons—prophetic statements of what their futures would be.

Of Reuben, his father said, *"Reuben, you are my firstborn; my might and the beginning of my strength, preeminent in dignity and preeminent in power"* (Genesis 49:3).

Then Jacob added this rebuke: *"Uncontrolled as water, you shall not have preeminence, because you went up to your father's bed; then you defiled it"* (v.4).

Think of water. It has no self-discipline or ability to hold itself in check and must be contained within another vessel.

Instead of receiving a double portion, Reuben's birthright was given to Joseph (1 Chronicles 5:1). What a sad ending to such a promising life.

SON NUMBER TWO:
SIMEON

Much to Rachel's chagrin, Leah was pregnant for the second time. Into the world came Simeon—whose name signifies "hearing," or "one who hears."

In the words of Leah, *"Because the Lord has heard that I am unloved. He has therefore given me this son also"* (Genesis 29:33).

Please notice it is the *woman* who is giving the names to the twelve sons of Israel—and what she calls them gives us an insight into her own condition.

Now we are in the second stage of our spiritual development. First we are Reubens, newborn sons and daughters of God. We don't receive all of our blessings at the beginning, but we have amazing potential. However, it takes time on our knees before we learn to clearly hear the voice of God.

A TWO-WAY CONVERSATION

We often hear the phrase, "God told me to do this," or "The Lord told me to say this to you."

Well, how did God speak? Did you hear an audible voice? Very few do. For most of us it is an inner hearing which is accompanied by a calm assurance. It takes prayerful practice and experience to truly know the voice of God versus the lying voice of the deceiver who tries to influence our thoughts.

Jesus declared, *"My sheep hear my voice"* (John 10:27). We are also told that solid spiritual food *"is for the mature, who because of practice have their senses trained to discern good and evil"* (Hebrews 5:14).

As we hear the Lord direct us, we begin to walk in His ways and develop a communion with Him. It's a two-way conversation. God's ears are open and He is listening to our prayers.

Remember, *"...the eyes of the Lord...run to and fro through the whole earth"* (Zechariah 4:10). He is seeking those who love Him and He is accessible to us.

I've heard it said, "We've got to bombard heaven!" I really don't think that's the right approach. God is more anxious to hear your heartfelt prayer than you are to speak it. His ears are always open—24/7.

As we spend time in His presence, we hear Him speaking to us. This is why we are cautioned not to become *"dull of hearing"* (Hebrews 5:11).

REFUSING TO LISTEN?

Some of us, because we really don't want to face ourselves and are not willing to change, pretend we don't hear the Lord when He speaks to our hearts:

- "I want you to watch your tongue."
- "I want you to love your husband."
- "I want you to spend time in My Word."
- "I want to have fellowship with you in prayer."

The Lord warns us not to *"harden your hearts"* as the children of Israel did (Psalm 95:8). Because of their unbelief, the Lord didn't allow them to enter into the Promised Land (v.11).

Even though we are blood-washed children of God, in certain areas we are reluctant or even refuse to hear what the Father is saying. As a result we are short-changed and will not have the rest and peace God wants to give us. This occurs primarily within our soul realm—our mind, will and emotions.

Some Christians question why they are so depressed and anxious. It may be because they have become "spiritually deaf"—refusing to listen to what the Almighty is saying and failing to acknowledge His Lordship.

While such people may make heaven, think of the blessings they will forfeit. Jesus says, *"Take my yoke upon you and learn from Me, for I am gentle and humble in heart, and you will find rest for your souls"* (Matthew 11:29).

In addition, we women have to face one challenge that men don't. For most of us, there is at least one week out of each month when it is just impossible to get along with anyone who comes near us. They are all just horrible, purposely trying to drive us crazy. Besides that, absolutely *everything* in our lives is going wrong, wrong, wrong!! *Nothing* is right and *nobody* understands!

But let me assure you, God has provided light at the end of that tunnel. He understands and cares about the unique problems of females. Even in the Garden of Eden, He spoke of it and tenderly promised help. The presence of the Comforter and Healer can carry us through any physical and emotional upheavals. There is rest for body and soul—the mind, will and emotions.

SON NUMBER THREE:
LEVI

It happened again! Leah presented a third son to Jacob. She called him Levi—which means "attachment" or "joined."

The name is significant to Leah because when he was born, she said, *"Now this time my husband will become attached to me, because I have borne him three sons"* (Genesis 29:34).

What was she referring to? Of course she and Jacob were married and joined legally and physically, yet up until this point there had been no spiritual, loving attachment—what today's psychologists call "bonding."

Avenging a Sister's Honor

We are discussing Jacob's sons, but did you know he and Leah also had a daughter named Dinah? In those days women didn't inherit property so she could not be given land to lead one of the tribes.

This is a tragic story which involves disobedience on Jacob's part. You see, the Lord had told him to go back to Bethel, yet he remained in a Canaanite area. It was during this time his daughter, Dinah, was exposed to wicked influences.

Like any young woman, she wanted to hang out with her peers. The Bible says she *"went out to visit the daughters of the land"* (Genesis 34:1).

It wasn't a wise move. The local prince of the area, Shechem, raped her. At least the man behaved with more honor than expected, because he wanted to marry Dinah!

When Simeon and Levi heard the news, they were livid—and met with Shechem's father, Hamor. They were ready to avenge the dignity and honor of their full-blooded sister.

A Deceitful Proposal

Hamor, who was in charge of the city, explained how much his son loved Dinah and his people would do *anything* if there could be a wedding. He even offered, *"Intermarry with us, give us your daughters and take our daughters for yourselves"* (v.9).

At that moment, Simeon and Levi made a deceitful proposal, saying, *"We cannot do this thing, to give our sister to one who is uncircumcised, for that would be a disgrace to us. Only on this condition will we consent to you: if you will become like us, in that every male of you be circumcised"* (vv.14-15).

Hamor and Shechem readily agreed and brought every man in the city to be circumcised. Three days later, *"when they were in pain"* (v.25) from the procedure and not able to move, Simeon and Levi came in with their swords raised and killed every male in the city—including Hamor and Shechem. It was a vicious, deceitful crime, but they rescued Dinah in the process.

Later, Jacob would say of Simeon and Levi, *"Their swords are implements of violence...Cursed be their anger, for it is fierce; and their wrath, for it is cruel. I will disperse them...and scatter them in Israel"* (Genesis 49:5-7).

This is an eye-opening lesson of what can happen when we expose our children to wicked influence because of our own disobedience.

The Transformation

Now for the rest of the story. Even though Levi committed a grievous act, his descendants would become the priestly tribe of Israel—the Levites—representing God before man.

In his earlier days, Levi was as wild and untamed as any young man could be. He must have experienced deep repentance, because God transformed both him and his tribe into spiritual leaders. This is an example of what the Lord can do with any who choose to "join" with Him.

Four generations later, when Moses pronounced a blessing on the tribes of Israel, here is what he declared concerning the Levites: *"...they have observed thy word, and kept thy covenant. They shall teach Jacob thy judgments, and Israel thy law: they shall put incense before thee, and whole burnt sacrifice upon thine altar. Bless, Lord, his substance, and accept the work of his hands"* (Deuteronomy 22:8-11 KJV).

These blessings can be ours as we are joined with the Father and accept the responsibility of representing God before men.

Son Number Four:

Judah

The fourth child born to Jacob and Leah was called Judah—meaning "praise." Scripture tells us, *"And she conceived again and bore a son and said, 'This time I will praise the Lord.' Therefore she named him Judah. Then she stopped bearing"* (Genesis 29:35).

The parallel progression of our own spiritual development continues this pattern—from being born again, hearing the voice of the Lord, becoming truly bonded to God, and now learning a new dimension—praising Him.

After the physical and spiritual joining, true praise can begin to flow from our lives. And, as we move in the Spirit, we become one with Him—leading us into a deeper dimension.

In the Old Testament when the tribe of Judah went to war, they would send a "praise band" ahead of the armies. Just before one battle, the leader, *"...appointed those who sang to the Lord and those who praised Him in holy attire, as they went out before the army and said, "Give thanks to the Lord, for His lovingkindness is everlasting.' When they began singing and praising, the Lord set ambushes against the sons of Ammon, Moab and Mount Seir, who had come against Judah; so they were routed"* (2 Chronicles 10:21-22).

What amazing miracles praise can bring!

In these last days, the Holy Spirit has opened the understanding of praise to the church in a phenomenal way. In recent years, numerous anointed books and tapes spread like wildfire throughout the world. Believers' lives have been changed dramatically when they learned what it meant to simply praise God. And there are astounding testimonies of believers miraculously delivered from danger as they praised the Lord.

"God Meant it For Good"

Sadly, the man who represented this glorious dimension of praise, fell into immorality in his life. Genesis 38 describes the sordid story of how he slept with his daughter-in-law, Tamar, and sired two illegitimate sons.

In addition, it seems there was a mercenary quality in his character. When we look at the story of Joseph about to be killed by his jealous brothers, it was Judah who suggested, *"'What profit is it for us to kill our brother and cover up his blood? Come and let us sell him to the Ishmaelites and not lay our hands on him, for he is our brother, our own flesh.' And his brothers listened to him"* (Genesis 37:26-27).

Now in fairness to Judah, that may have been a ploy to protect Joseph from the brothers' vicious rage. But it sounds rather like: "Hey, guys! If we are going to kill the little varmint, let's at least get some money out of it!"

Some brotherly love!

But 22 years later, as the brothers stood before "Governor" Joseph in Egypt, they heard him utter the words which have been called one of the most noble pieces of natural eloquence in any literature: *"But as for you, ye thought evil against me; but God meant it unto good"* (Genesis 50:20 KJV).

Faced with the revelation of their character and deeds,

Judah acknowledged the guilt of their actions and pled with Joseph to take him and let him be responsible instead of Benjamin.

Judah was offering to take someone else's place. Sound familiar? He was an Old Testament type of Christ. You see, a marvelous change happened in his life. From his immoral and mercenary past, the Almighty had transformed him into a genuine man of God.

His older brothers, Reuben, Simeon and Levi, had each forfeited the birthright. But Judah/Praise now lived up to his name—qualified to be entrusted in that position, with earthly and spiritual authority.

"TO THE TENTH GENERATION"

Years later, Jacob's blessing over this special son included these words: *"Judah, your brothers shall praise you"* (Genesis 49:8).

But perhaps the most important prophetic word Jacob declared concerning Judah was when he said, *"The scepter* [rod] *shall not depart from Judah, nor the ruler's staff from between his feet, until Shiloh comes, and to him shall be the obedience of the peoples"* (v.10).

Seven hundred years later, the Lord Jesus Christ came from the tribe of Judah—not from the descendants of any of Jacob's eleven other sons. Scripture tells us, *"Stop weeping; behold, the Lion that is from the tribe of Judah, the Root of David, has overcome"* (Revelation 5:5).

The Scepter extending to the tenth generation—or

700 years—is significant because of Jacob's sin with his daughter-in-law. Scripture says, *"No one of illegitimate birth shall enter the assembly of the Lord; none of his descendants, even to the tenth generation"* (Deuteronomy 23:2). The past was cleansed!

Shiloh means "rest"—and Jesus declares, *"Come to me, all who are weary and heavy-laden, and I will give you rest"* (Matthew 11:28).

Remember, when the children of Israel prepared to enter the Promised Land, it was the tribe of Judah who crossed Jordan first. So it is with us. It is praise that will precede our entering into a promised land of rest from the wanderings and battles of life. Selah!

SON NUMBER FIVE:
DAN

When Rachel was unable to conceive, she became so envious of her sister, she could no longer contain herself rationally. She did exactly what most of us do when we find ourselves in an intensely frustrating situation. We blame somebody else! It must have been a sight to behold when she ranted at Jacob: *"Give me children, or else I die"* (Genesis 30:1).

Jacob angrily retaliated, *"Am I in the place of God, who has withheld from you the fruit of the womb?"* (v.2).

Probably stung by the truth of his reproof, she backed

off and devised an alternative plan to get what she wanted.

Rachel suggested a plan common in that day—surrogate motherhood: *"Here is my maid Bilhah, go in to her that she may bear on my knees, that through her I too may have children"* (v.3).

In those days, the son of a handmaid was considered the legal son of the wife, with all the rights and privileges.

When Bilhah conceived and bore Jacob a son, Rachel proudly exclaimed, *" 'God has vindicated me, and has indeed heard my voice and has given me a son. Therefore she named him Dan"* (v.6).

It was almost bragging—insisting others acknowledge that she too was worthy to bear children, and God had passed judgment in her favor. Now she also could present Jacob with a son. She named this child Dan, which means "judge."

THE KEY TO LIBERTY

Today, as we grow in God, we begin to comprehend the many facets and characteristics of the Father, and one of them is His position as judge over all things.

In scripture, judgment includes deliverance. As God told the children of Israel, *"I am the Lord, and I will bring you out from under the burdens of the Egyptians, and I will deliver you from their bondage I will also redeem you with an outstretched arm and with great judgments"* (Exodus 6:6).

We come to a point in the Christian walk when His righteous decrees are pronounced over our lives. Our heavenly authority will say, "Those things which have bound you will bind you no more. I am setting you free!"

Even though we are guilty, we can be delivered because He is both our Judge and Advocate.

"My Advocate"

Let me share these words written by Martha Snell Nicholson which dramatically portray the adequacy of Christ's atoning work on the Cross. It is titled, "My Advocate."

I sinned. And straightway, posthaste, Satan flew
Before the presence of the most High God,
And made a railing accusation there.
He said, "This soul, this thing of clay and sod,
Has sinned. 'Tis true that he has named Thy Name,
But I demand his death, for Thou has said,
'The soul that sinneth, it shall die.'"

Shall not Thy sentence be fulfilled? Is justice dead?
Send now this wretched sinner to his doom.
What other thing can righteous ruler do?"
And thus he did accuse me day and night,

And every word he spoke, O God, was true!
Then quickly One rose up from God's right hand,

Before whose glory angels veiled their eyes.
He spoke, "Each jot and tittle of the law
Must be fulfilled; the guilty sinner dies!

But wait—suppose his guilt were all transferred
To Me, and that I paid his penalty!
Behold My hands, My side, My feet! One day
I was made sin for him, and died that he
Might be presented faultless at Thy throne!"
And Satan fled away. Full well he knew
That he could not prevail against such love,
For every word my dear Lord spoke was true!

Praise the Lord! Our Judge is also our Advocate—and He vindicates us. It is our heritage as children of God.

YOUR TRIUMPH

Knowing this aspect of our Father's character we can overcome *anything*—regardless of our past.

The Amplified Bible sheds this light on Isaiah 54:17: *"But no weapon that is formed against you shall prosper, and every tongue that shall rise against you in judgment you shall show to be in the wrong. This* [peace, righteousness, security, triumph over opposition] *is the heritage of the servants of the Lord* [those in whom the ideal Servant of the Lord is reproduced]; *this is the righteousness or the vindication which they obtain from*

Me [this is that which I impart to them as their justification], *says the Lord."*

Eventually the tribe of Dan would fulfill their name in having an important judicial function in the future nation of Israel. When we read the story of Samson, we learn he was a Danite (Judges 13:2) and judged the nation for 20 years.

SON NUMBER SIX:
NAPHTALI

Once more, Rachel turned to her maid, Bilhah, to do what she couldn't; produce a son for Jacob. He was given the name Naphtali—which means "to wrestle."

Rachel wasn't being complimentary to Leah when she said, *"With mighty wrestlings I have wrestled with my sister and I have indeed prevailed"* (Genesis 30:8).

Here was this natural beauty who was probably as cute as a button. She knew Jacob loved her and they probably laughed together at poor Leah who was becoming more unattractive as time marched on. By boasting, *"I have indeed prevailed,"* there's not much in Rachel's character to recommend her, in spite of her good looks!

THE WARFARE CONTINUES

After we have taken on the best traits of Reuben,

Simeon, Levi, Judah and Dan, we begin to understand that wrestling is a spiritual reality. God's Word tells us, *"For we wrestle not against flesh and blood, but against principalities, against powers, against the rulers of the darkness of this world, against spiritual wickedness in high places"* (Ephesians 6:12 KJV)

This is why we are told to put on *"the full armor of God, so that you will be able to resist in the evil day, and having done everything, to stand firm"* (v.13).

If any part of our armor is missing, Satan will seize his opportunity to attack.

There is also a wrestling that takes place with God. In Jacob's younger days, he tried to make bargains with the Lord: "If you will do this, I will serve you." For example, after his dream at Bethel, Jacob said, *"If God will be with me and will keep me on this journey that I take, and will give me food to eat and garments to wear, and I return to my father's house in safety, then the Lord will be my God"* (Genesis 28:20-21).

Obviously, he wasn't a spiritual giant at that time. But after many difficult and painful experiences, Jacob finally became honest with himself.

GOD KNOWS!

In our time of wrestling, we try to hide our weaknesses, since we don't want the Lord to know what we are truly like on the inside. Yet He knows!

Psalm 139:1-4 says it well: *"O Lord, you have*

searched me and you know me. You know when I sit and when I rise; you perceive my thoughts from afar. You discern my going out and my lying down; you are familiar with all my ways. Before a word is on my tongue you know it completely."

Jacob's great turn-around came during his wrestling match with the angel. What God was trying to have Jacob admit was that he was—a "cheater," a sinner.

Only when we stand naked before the Lord, admit who we truly are and confess our needs, will He change us. Otherwise we will be running from ourselves forever—pretending our iniquity is not there. And He can never use us effectively because our flesh keeps getting in the way.

SON NUMBER SEVEN:

GAD

Earlier, after Leah gave birth to her fourth son, Judah, the Bible says *"she stopped bearing"* (Genesis 29:35).

Yet, looking at how Rachel solved the motherhood problem, she decided to take the same route and gave her maid, Zilpah, to Jacob so another child could be born who would be legally hers. When a son from their union entered the world, Leah said, *"'How fortunate!' So she named him Gad"* (Genesis 30:11).

When the children of Israel were going into the Promised Land under Joshua (Numbers 32), the tribes of

Reuben and Gad (and the half-tribe of Joseph's son, Manasseh) stayed on the east side of the Jordan river—not the west side where the blessings were.

This is a telling picture of only entering half way into what God has for us.

Several centuries later, when Jesus journeyed through this same region, *"...into the country of the Gadarenes"* (Mark 5:1 KJV), He encountered a demonic.

The man had been dwelling among the tombs and no one was able to restrain him, not even with a chain because *"...the chains had been torn apart by him and the shackles broken in pieces, and no one was strong enough to subdue him"* (v.4).

When the demon-possessed man saw Jesus, he came running up and bowed before Him, shouting with a loud voice, *"What business do we have with each other, Jesus, Son of the Most High God? I implore You by God, do not torment me!"* (v.7).

Jesus had been saying to him, *"Come out of the man, you unclean spirit!"* (v.8).

"What is your name?" the Lord asked the demonic. He answered, *"My name is Legion; for we are many"* (v.9).

THE DROWNING PIGS

The men in this region were swine herders and there was a large herd of pigs feeding nearby on the side of the mountain.

The demons in the possessed man implored Jesus, *"Send us into the swine so that we may enter them"* (v.12).

What happened next is one of the most amazing events in the ministry of Jesus. He gave the demons permission, *"And coming out, the unclean spirits entered the swine; and the herd rushed down the steep bank into the sea, about two thousand of them; and they were drowned in the sea"* (v.13).

Miraculously, the man who had a "legion" of demons was now *"...sitting down, clothed and in his right mind"* (v.15).

It is significant that the children of Israel were not to deal with swine, but the descendants of Gad, who had only entered half way into God's promises were raising pigs, and became open targets for the works of the devil.

It's an important lesson to learn—going only half-way in the things of God will result in more problems down the line.

Son Number Eight:

Asher

Once more, Leah turned to her maid Zilpha to conceive a child with Jacob. She bore a second son, who Leah named Asher—or "joy filled"— because Leah said, *"Happy am I! For women will call me happy"* (Genesis 30:3).

What a pleasure to be in the company of a woman who lets the presence of the Lord radiate through her. And we know without a shadow of a doubt her joy is genuine.

Before Moses died, he took time to bless the children of Israel and had a special word for Asher. He said, *"More blessed than sons is Asher; may he be favored by his brothers, and may he dip his foot in oil"* (Deuteronomy 33:24).

The geography of the tribe of Asher is shaped like a graceful foot, a territory which extended from near Mount Carmel in the south to near Tyre in the north (Joshua 19:24-31).

The Flow of Oil

There are many who believe, prophetically, that vast quantities of oil will be found in this region, which will produce great wealth for present day Israel.

The oil of Asher also speaks of the anointing of the Holy Spirit, which comes after we progress through the stages of our spiritual development which mirror the lives of the sons of Israel.

When you enter into the presence of God's Spirit, prepare for the unexpected! When Moses came down from meeting with God on the mountain, the Bible says, *"...Moses did not know that the skin of his face shone because of his speaking with Him"* (Exodus 34:29).

The glow was so powerful Moses had to place a veil

over his face when he spoke to the people (v.35).

When we have a personal encounter with the Lord, we will be the kind of individual others like to be around: filled with the joy of the Lord!

SON NUMBER NINE:

ISSACHAR

So far, Jacob had eight sons by three different women—four from Leah and two each from the handmaidens, Bilhah and Zilpha.

It had been quite some time since Leah conceived, and she desperately desired more children.

One day, during the time of the wheat harvest, Reuben found some mandrakes—plants which give off a sweet smell. They were considered an aphrodisiac, and helpful in promoting conception. The Hebrew word for them is "love apples."

After he brought them home for his mother Leah, Rachel asked her, "Please, could I have some of your mandrakes?"

Leah retorted bitterly, *"Is it a small matter for you to take my husband? And would you take my son's mandrakes also?"* (Genesis 30:15).

So Rachel bargained with her and said, *"Therefore he may lie with you tonight in return for your son's mandrakes"* (v.15).

That evening, when Jacob came home from the fields,

Leah was waiting for him. *"'You must come in to me, for I have surely hired you with my son's mandrakes.' So he lay with her that night"* (v.16).

God was listening to Leah, and she became pregnant and gave Jacob a fifth son by her. She said, *"God has given me my wages because I gave my maid to my husband"* (v.18).

Leah named her son Issachar—"man of hire" or "He will bring reward." She was saying, "God has given me my wages because of what I have given to my husband."

The Bible deals with practical matters and there is much written concerning hiring and wages. In the New Testament, Jesus used many such examples in His parables.

Issachar was a man who knew what it meant to work. He understood we have to earn our wages. The principle began in Eden when God said man would have to earn his bread by the sweat of his brow. Nobody gets anything for nothing. The New Testament puts it this way, "If anyone won't work, neither will he eat." It's that simple.

Jacob in his prophecies concerning his sons, likened Issachar to a *"strong donkey"* bearing heavy burdens. (Genesis 49:14)

As we mature in Christ, we learn how to carry the weight of trials and tribulations.

Isachar was both physical and practical and God would give him a pleasant land in which to dwell (v.15).

SON NUMBER TEN:
ZEBULUN

Leah became pregnant once more and had a child named Zebulun—his name denotes "habitation" or "dwelling place."

She said, *"God has endowed me with a good gift; now my husband will dwell with me, because I have borne him six sons"* (Genesis 30:20).

As we come to this level of development in Christ we begin to know what it means for the Lord to dwell in us and for us to live in His presence.

What a confidence is ours when we are secure in the knowledge God is ever present—and we are part of the temple built up with stones *"fitly joined together"* (Ephesians 4:16 KJV).

We are the Lord's dwelling place and He inhabits the praises of His people (Psalm 22:3).

We now understand the meaning of "Christ in us, the hope of glory," and we can joyfully sing, "He walks with me and He talks with me..."

In Jacob's blessing, he said, *"Zebulun will dwell at the seashore; and he shall be a haven for ships"* (Genesis 49:13)—in other words, he would have contact with the outside world.

On our spiritual journey, only after we come to the place of dwelling in God's presence are we capable of providing a harbor for others.

Son Number Eleven:
Joseph

Could it be, that after all these years, Rachel would personally conceive and have a son?

It was true! And into the world came Joseph.

Even though Rachel didn't have much to commend her character, she had enough sense to know the Lord always has more in store for His children.

At Joseph's birth, she proclaimed, *"God has taken away my reproach"* (Genesis 30:23). His name means "fruitful," or in Rachel's words, *"May the Lord give me another son"* (v.24).

Jacob referred to this in his blessing when he said, *"Joseph is a fruitful bough, a fruitful bough by a spring; it's branches run over a wall"* (Genesis 49:22).

This is a glimpse of both the strength of his character and the wide influence he enjoyed—even rising to power in another nation.

Of course, Joseph was assaulted by his enemies, but God prevailed and protected him. *"The archers bitterly attacked him, and shot at him and harassed him; but his bow remained firm, and his arms were agile, from the hands of the Mighty One of Jacob (From there is the Shepherd, the Stone of Israel)"* (vv.23-24)

In just one verse (25), the word "blesses" or "blessings" is mentioned five time—which underscores the fact that Joseph would experience success greater than all of his brothers.

This is quite a transformation from Joseph as a young man, when he didn't exercise wisdom. He wore his coat of many colors and chattered on about his dreams where everyone bowed down to him. Even his parents scolded him for that one!

It seems he was either oblivious to his brothers' envy and resentment or didn't care. No wonder they hated him!

Yet the Lord eventually fulfilled His promise and made him an esteemed leader. God's goodness far exceeds our dreams. He is *"...able to do exceeding abundantly above all that we ask or think"* (Ephesians 3:20 KJV).

Regardless of the spiritual level we are currently on, He can raise us to new heights.

When Jacob took away Reuben's birthright because of sin (1 Chronicles 5:1), it was given to none other than Joseph.

SON NUMBER TWELVE:
BENJAMIN

In case you're counting, Leah had six natural sons, plus two by her handmaid. Rachel personally bore one son, and two by her maid.

To whom would the final leader of the tribes of Israel be born? It was Rachel.

While on a journey from Bethel to Ephrath

(Bethlehem), Rachel went into labor, but had great difficulty. Her midwife said to her, *"Do not fear, for now you have another son"* Genesis 35:18).

However, during the delivery, just before she knew she was going to die, Rachel named the boy "Ben-oni"—or "son of my sorrow." But Jacob changed his name to Benjamin—"son of my right hand."

Rachel was buried on the way to what is now the city of Bethlehem.

A PLACE OF HONOR

In the Bible, the right hand consistently refers to the power and glory of God. The psalmist writes, *"His right hand and His holy arm have gained the victory for Him"* (Psalm 98:1) and *"In Your right hand there are pleasures forever"* (Psalm 98:1).

Even in today's protocol, to be seated at the right hand of someone is an important honor. With world leaders, this place is often reserved for a trusted confidant.

Jesus, following His death, burial and resurrection, ascended to heaven and is now seated at the right hand of the Father (Hebrews 12:2).

This brings us to the final stage of our development, from Reuben (being born again) to Benjamin (being rewarded with a place of honor by the Father). Now we are God's right hand on earth, bringing deliverance to the people around us.

The sons and mothers of Israel left a legacy which has spanned generations and left an indelible impact on our world.

Many wonder if, after Rachel's death, there was ever a rekindling of love between Jacob and Leah. The Bible does not reveal this specifically, however it was Leah who was buried alongside of Jacob.

Her eyes may have been weak, but Leah was focused on the Lord, and was graciously rewarded.

CHAPTER 4

*T*EN WOMEN WORTH EMULATING

*W*hen I began to seriously study God's Word, I was amazed to see how the Lord used women in His master plan—from Genesis to Revelation. And the closer I looked the more I realized that the Almighty didn't choose women with only certain characteristics or talents, or because they were more spiritual, smarter, or somehow better than others. No, God used *every* person with their own unique abilities—and faults.

Let me share with you ten specific women in the Bible, along with the meaning of their names.

Understanding the names in Scripture is important, because they reveal the character, work and purpose of an individual. That's why the angel instructed Joseph to call Mary's son, "Jesus" (salvation)—because He would save His people from their sins.

As we consider these ten individual women, we will see that God uses different personalities in different ways at different times. He may want to use you as one of these types. Or He may want you to be a little of all of them at various times, according to the need. Each of these women has certain characteristics worth emulating.

A wise person will follow the example of worthy role models. That's why God included them in Scripture—so we could learn from their lives, grow in the grace and knowledge of the Lord, and become prepared for whatever He may require of us.

1. Miriam
– A Worship Leader

The sister of Moses and Aaron—Miriam—played a pivotal role in the exodus of the children of Israel from Egypt. Around the time Moses was born, a decree was announced in the nation that all male Hebrew infants were to be killed. Worried for her child's safety, Jochebed, the mother, placed baby Moses in a basket on the river and asked Miriam to watch over him to make sure he was not harmed.

What an amazing story of Moses drifting downstream only to be found by Pharaoh's daughter. Miriam quickly approached her and offered to find a Hebrew nurse to help care for the baby. You guessed it. The nurse was little Moses' own mother!

After being by the side of Moses through the nine plagues, she and Aaron worked along side their brother during the exodus out of Egypt. When God spared the children of Israel by parting the Red Sea, it was Miriam who became the leader of worship and praise. The Bible records, *"Miriam the prophetess, Aaron's sister, took the timbrel in her hand, and all the women went out after her with timbrels and with dancing. Miriam answered them,*

> *'Sing to the Lord,*
> *for He is highly exalted;*
> *The horse and his rider*
> *He has hurled into the sea'"*
> (Exodus 15:20-21).

STRENGTH AND WEAKNESS

The meaning of Miriam's name in Hebrew is "bitter"—the root word is myrrh, an incense used in worship. It is the same root used when Naomi, the mother-in-law of Ruth, said, "Don't call me 'Naomi' (meaning pleasant); call me 'Mara' because the Almighty has dealt bitterly with me."

Worship leaders have a unique ministry, and it isn't musical talent or accomplishment that qualifies them. It takes being broken before the Lord, enduring some bitter hard times to truly comprehend His sustaining power. Learning to know God's presence in the midst of difficulties and bitterness works something deep in our

69

souls, and brings forth genuine worship. We must know this dimension before we are able to lead others into it.

Yet, Miriam had her weaknesses, including common human emotions such as jealousy and pride. Apparently she and Aaron disliked their sister-in-law. Talking about this matter together whipped their feelings into full-scale resentment of Moses' authority.

Sullenly, they murmured to each other, *"Has the Lord indeed spoken only through Moses? Has He not spoken through us as well?"* (Numbers 12:2).

God heard what was said and after chastising them, Miriam found herself suddenly plagued with leprosy.

Immediately, Moses and Aaron fell on their faces before the Lord and Moses cried out, *"O God, heal her, I pray!"* (v.13).

The Lord responded, yet Miriam had to remain in this condition for seven days outside the camp before the leprosy was completely healed and the people could move on. It was a humiliating punishment.

Interestingly, they were camped at Hazeroth which means "walled in" when this took place. After Miriam was fully recovered, they moved to Paran—which means "making oneself beautiful."

TRIALS AND TRIUMPHS

The lesson we need to learn from Miriam's failure is that by allowing wrong attitudes to fester and grow, we affect and influence the lives of those around us—our families and fellow believers. The result often being we cause others to become hemmed in, unable to move toward the land God has promised.

The Lord restored Miriam, "the prophetess" to ministry and leadership. She once again was "something beautiful" and remained together with her brothers for the next 40 years through trials and triumphs.

2. HULDAH
– SPEAKING GOD'S WORD

A little-known but important woman in the Old Testament is Huldah—and the Lord used her in a mighty way to deliver a message to Hilkiah, the high priest, and to Josiah the king.

The king and the priest knew they had a problem. When the temple in Jerusalem was being repaired, they found The Book of the Law which had been ignored for several years. And when Josiah read it, he was frightened because he knew his people were practicing gross idolatry, and he realized the prophesied judgment would come crashing down upon his head!

Scripture tells us they sought out a woman named Huldah, who understood the law, and asked her about the writings. When the high priest and his group arrived at her house, she bluntly told them, *"Tell the man who sent you to me, thus says the Lord, 'Behold, I bring evil on this place and on its inhabitants, even all the words of the book which the king of Judah has read. Because they have forsaken Me and have burned incense to other gods that they might provoke Me to anger with all the work of their hands, therefore My wrath burns against this place, and it shall not be quenched'"* (2 Kings 22:15-17).

What a sobering message!

A VOICE OF THE LORD

Huldah's name in Hebrew has two meanings. One is "battle maid" or "woman of strength." The other is "weasel," representing the smooth "gliding motion" of the little animal. The two meanings together present the image of a very strong, yet graceful woman.

From what biblical historians tell us, she was an intellectual, probably a teacher or librarian at a religious school. Scripture also states she was a prophetess (v.14), who spoke the word of God to the nation.

You and I can become the voice of the Lord to our world. The Bible says, *"If any man speak, let him speak as the oracles of God; if any man minister, let him do it as of the ability which God giveth: that God in all things may be glorified through Jesus Christ, to whom be praise and dominion for ever and ever"* (1 Peter 4:11 KJV).

As believers we need to discipline ourselves and not allow every thought which enters our mind to come tumbling out of our mouth. Ask the Lord to guard your thought life and to give you the right words to say—at the right time.

Huldah, the "battle maid," is a prime example. She

communicated under God's control and there was an *ease*—a smoothness to the manner in which she spoke on behalf of the Lord. Though extremely strong, she was lady-like and gracious—never harsh, shrieking, or unpleasant in her demeanor.

3. DEBORAH
– GENTLE, YET STRONG

Who says God doesn't want women to occupy places of authority? Of course He does, just take a look at the history of Deborah.

She was both a professional woman and a judge of Israel—which meant a position of great honor and elevated power. People came to her for decisions which would affect the entire society.

The root of her name is "bee" or "wasp." (That's easy to remember by thinking of the nickname for Deborah— "Deb-bee.")

Bees are among the most focused and industrious of God's creatures. They produce honey—a marvelous substance with numerous benefits for health. And they pollinate vegetation all around them—causing new growth and ongoing sustenance for others. But a bee's sting can be deadly!

"I Will Surely Go"

Deborah's name is also appropriate, since the enemies of Israel, the Canaanites, certainly felt her sting! When she instructed the military general, Barak to lead 10,000 soldiers in battle at Mount Tabor, he responded quite wisely, *"If you will go with me, then I will go; but if you will not go with me, I will not go"* (Judges 4:8).

Barak was sharp! He knew God was with this woman and if she were present, victory would be theirs. Deborah answered, *"I will surely go with you; nevertheless, the honor shall not be yours on the journey that you are about to take, for the Lord will sell Sisera* [the cruel commander of the Canaanites armies] *into the hands of a woman"* (v.9).

At a critical point, when all the enemy armies had gathered, Deborah gave the order, "Charge!"—*"For this is the day in which the Lord has given Sisera into your hands; behold, the Lord has gone out before you"* (v.14).

The vast army of the Canaanites were routed, but somehow Sisera managed to escape on foot to the tent of a woman named Jael, the wife of Heber, where he thought he would be safe. She invited him in, offered a beverage, covered him with a rug and assured him, "Don't be afraid."

Thinking she was an ally, Sisera said to her, *"Stand in the doorway of the tent, and it shall be if anyone comes and inquires of you, and says, 'Is there anyone here?' that you shall say, 'No'"* (v.20).

However, Jael had another plan. Scripture records

that when he fell asleep, she *"...took a tent peg and seized a hammer in her hand, and went secretly to him and drove the peg into his temple, and it went through into the ground"* (v.21). So was the demise of Sisera.

It came from the hand of a woman, just as Deborah prophesied; and after the war she led Israel during a time of peace which lasted for 40 years.

Women like Deborah—certain in their purpose and knowledge of God—are a worthy role model, respected at all levels of society, even by mighty warriors.

4. ANNA
– AN INTERCESSOR

In the temple at Jerusalem there was a woman named Anna who waited perhaps 70 years for the promised Messiah. Can you imagine her excitement when Mary and Joseph brought young Jesus to be dedicated?

Look at how the Bible describes that day. *"And there was a prophetess, Anna the daughter of Phanuel, of the tribe of Asher. She was advanced in years and had lived with her husband seven years after her marriage, and then as a widow to the age of eighty-four. She never left the temple, serving night and day with fastings and prayers. At that very moment she came up and began giving thanks to God, and continued to speak of Him to all those who were looking for the redemption of Jerusalem"* (Luke 2:36-38).

Anna became a devoted intercessor in prayer and spent her days and nights seeking God. Her name means "favored" and she came from the tribe of Asher, which means "bright and happy."

Even though Anna was elderly, I believe she had a cheerful personality and was pleasant company. And now, what joy she must have experienced when the Messiah appeared before her very eyes. Every moment she had spent in prayer was now rewarded.

Touching the Heart of God

We need millions of Anna's in our world—women who have a ministry of intercession.

I think about the widow who can only make it to church when someone is kind enough to pick her up and drive her to the house of God. Yet, I see the same woman alone in her home, taking the morning newspaper and spreading it out on the floor, earnestly praying:

- "Lord, minister to this family whose home was burned to the ground."
- "God, I pray for this mother whose child was murdered yesterday. Let your Spirit come and comfort her as only you can."
- "Father, I bring before you these women who have been raped in our community—and they can't find the culprit behind these horrible acts. I am asking Your Spirit to reveal that person. Uncover the works of darkness. Bring

about justice and healing to these victims.

Oh for intercessors, people behind the scenes, obscure to the limelight, yet they touch the very heart of God.

5. MARY
– A LIFE OF OBEDIENCE

The mother of Jesus was given a name which has the same root word as Miriam—*myrrh*. She too would taste bitter things in her life, including the terrible death of her Son.

Mary was a simple peasant, yet one of her most outstanding qualities was her devout obedience to the Word of the Lord. There was no one more surprised than Mary when an angel appeared to her and announced, *"...behold, you will conceive in your womb and bear a son, and you shall name Him Jesus. He will be great and will be called the Son of the Most High; and the Lord God will give Him the throne of His father David; and He will reign over the house of Jacob forever, and His kingdom will have no end"* (Luke 1:31-33).

Perplexed, Mary replied to the angel, *"How can this be, since I am a virgin?"* (v.34).

After the angel explained what would happen, she uttered one of the most profound statements in scripture. She said, *"Behold...may it be done to me according to your word"* (v.38).

Later, when her Son grew to be a Man and attended the wedding at Cana, Mary said to those around her, *"Whatever He says to you, do it"* (John 2:5). She recognized the power of Jesus.

Every time we see Mary it is a demonstration of obedience. For example, after the resurrection she was in the Upper Room with the 120 believers. Why? Because Jesus had said, *"And, behold, I send the promise of my Father upon you: but tarry ye in the city of Jerusalem, until ye be endued with power from on high"* (Luke 24:49 KJV).

We would do well to learn from Mary. Obedience to the Word of God is always the right thing to do—in every situation.

GOD IS ALWAYS AT WORK

Remember, in the very beginning, when Mary presented her Son to the Lord, Simeon blessed them and said to her, *"Behold, this Child is appointed for the fall and rise of many in Israel, and for a sign to be opposed—and a sword will pierce even your own soul"* (Luke 2:24-25).

There's bitterness again. But remember the Bible speaks about *"kicking against the pricks"* (Acts 26:14 KJV). This speaks of a disobedient ox or mule that kicks belligerently when it is pricked or prodded toward an action. In today's language, it means resisting the workings of God in your life, and "kicking" against what He wants you to do.

In those times when, spiritually, you feel you are walking around with a sword in your side, remember the Lord is still at work. He may be molding you into a Mary—an individual who knows how to listen and yield to the Word of God.

The Father will bring forth Jesus Christ to those around you even though you feel ill-equipped for such an assignment. Your education or status in life is immaterial, because in God's sight the only requirement is to be obedient to His calling.

6. LYDIA
– SHARING GOD'S ROYALTY

The apostle Paul and his co-workers were in Philippi, a leading city in the district of Macedonia. On the Sabbath, they walked down to the riverside where a woman named Lydia was conducting a prayer meeting—and they were not embarrassed or hesitant to join the women in prayer.

Lydia was a prominent businesswoman whose name means "a beautiful plain." Picture a productive field with rich golden wheat waving gently in the breeze. You know the harvest will prosper the owner and provide sustenance to many.

The Bible tells us this about her: *"A woman named Lydia, from the city of Thyatira, a seller of purple fabrics, a worshiper of God, was listening; and the Lord opened her heart to respond to the things spoken by Paul. And when she and her household had been baptized, she urged us, saying, 'If you have judged me to be faithful to the Lord, come into my house and stay.' And she prevailed upon us"* (Acts 16:14-15).

In these two verses we see eight important facts concerning Lydia:

One: She was from Thyatiria.

Why there, not someplace else? In the Book of Revelation we find a message to the church at Thyatira, a body of believers with a unique personality. They were the church of whom God said, *"I know thy works...and the last to be more than the first"* (Revelation 2:19 KJV).

The Lord was saying, "You started out well and kept on going—and when you overcome I am going to give you the authority to rule over nations" (vv.26-28).

This typifies the kind of woman Lydia was.

Two: She was a seller of "purple fabrics."

What does the color purple represent? Royalty. Lydia was engaged in the business of providing cloth—to cover those around her in regal garments. Even more, she represented the King of Kings!

Three: Lydia was "a worshiper of God."

There is a difference between simply being born again and becoming a worshiper in Spirit and truth—and Lydia had learned this wonderful dimension.

Four: The Bible says she "was listening."

Lydia had her ears perked and attuned to what Paul said.

Isn't it curious that the Bible mentions such a small and seemingly obvious detail? Apparently this "hearing" thing is quite important to God.

In the book of Revelation, He says it eight different times, *"He that hath an ear, let him hear what the spirit is saying..."*

In today's world, more than ever, there is a cacophony of noise—voices, music, entertainment, appliances and communication of every imaginable sound that would fill our minds. It could drive us crazy at worst, and misdirect us at least, if we don't shut it out and listen for the voice of the Lord—the only source of truth and peace.

Five: "The Lord opened her heart to respond."

We can't just waltz into the things of God whenever we choose and expect instant divine knowledge and wisdom.

It is only when the Holy Spirit opens our hearts spiritually that we can respond and understand His will and His ways. That's why none of us can boast of anything. Whatever good things we may attain are always of Him.

Six: Lydia "and her household" were baptized.

Here was a professional woman who knew how to have her life and household in order—family and servants alike. They respected her and followed her in water baptism.

Seven: She was open and transparent.

Lydia invited an analysis and inspection of her life, saying to Paul and his associates, "If you have judged me to be faithful to the Lord, come into my house and stay."

How many of us would be confident and bold enough to publically announce, "Examine me"? Or as Paul declared, *"Be ye followers of me, even as I also am of Christ"* (1 Corinthians 11:1 KJV).

Eight: She "prevailed."

Two simple words, "She prevailed."

If we want to triumph in life, we can learn from Lydia. She saw results from her energy, efforts and prayers.

Lydia's disciplined, yet welcoming spirit, representing the royalty of God's Kingdom, is one each of us can follow. She invited Paul and the other believers to join her prayer meeting, and then graciously asked them into her home. It goes without saying she knew how to practice hospitality.

As a result of all these characteristics in her life, she prevailed, and was highly blessed of the Lord.

7. DORCAS
– SHARING HER TALENTS

In the costal city of Joppa lived a disciple of Christ

named Dorcas (also called Tabitha). The Bible tells us, *"...this woman was abounding with deeds of kindness and charity which she continually did"* (Acts 9:36).

Her name means "gazelle." It brings forth the image of those beautiful deer-like creatures with powerful haunches, yet with exquisite sensitivity, ready to leap into flight at the slightest sound or rustle in the grass.

Dorcas was a sensitive person such as this.

She was a creative and talented woman, plus a gifted seamstress. Sadly, however, Dorcas fell sick and died. Her friends washed her body and laid her to rest in an upper room.

Word spread that Peter was preaching in a nearby city and two men rushed to him, imploring, "Please, come to Joppa as quickly as you can."

When he arrived, *"...they brought him into the upper room; and all the widows stood beside him, weeping and showing all the tunics and garments that Dorcas used to make while she was with them"* (v.39).

But Peter sent the mourners out of the room. Then he knelt down, prayed, and turning to the body, said, *"'Tabitha, arise.' And she opened her eyes, and when she saw Peter, she sat up. And he gave her his hand and raised her up; and calling he saints and widows, he presented her alive"* (vv.40-41).

SURRENDER YOUR TALENTS

The Lord has gifted some people with creative

abilities and talents in areas such as art, music, design, writing, decorating and gardening. The list goes on—all the things which enhance our life and surroundings.

Of course, by their very nature, gifted people are usually sensitive and sometimes *oversensitive*. They can have difficulty relating to others because their feelings are easily hurt or they feel misunderstood.

They can also become enamored and obsessed with their own abilities.

But those who walk in the Holy Spirit, using their talent for the Lord, are a wonderful gift of God, wherever they may be.

Dorcas is a worthy role model. With her hands she crafted garments for others—her tender heart and generous spirit enriched their lives, and God raised her from the dead!

8. PHOEBE
– SHINING BRIGHTLY FOR THE LORD

Two verses written by Paul to the church at Rome reveal the attributes of a most interesting woman. He writes, *"I commend to you our sister Phoebe, who is a servant of the church which is at Cenchrea; that you receive her in the Lord in a manner worthy of the saints, and that you help her in whatever matter she may have need of you; for she herself has also been a helper of many, and of myself as well"* (Romans 16:1-2).

The name Phoebe is taken from the Greek word *phos,* the same root from which we get *phosphorus.* It means "bright" or "shining."

Paul said she was a *servant* of the church at Cenchrea. The Greek word servant is *diakonon*, or "deacon." In the early church, it was a recognized position of leadership. Today, different denominations have created differing job descriptions for the title "Deacon." But in any case, it entails serving and helping ministries.

The phrase *"a great help to many"* suggests she may have been a businesswoman who could provide for and protect believers through her public influence. The request to receive her with honor probably indicates that she herself carried his letter to the church at Rome.

She was a leader in her congregation—a shining light for the Lord. As Daniel wrote long ago, *"Those who have insight will shine brightly like the brightness of the expanse of heaven, and those who lead the many to righteousness, like the stars forever and ever"* (Daniel 12:3).

Phoebe was such a person, and we can follow her example.

9. PRISCILLA
– WORKING WITH HER HUSBAND

One of my feminine favorites in scripture is Priscilla. Here was a woman who faithfully ministered with her husband, Aquila. Paul had an instant affinity with this couple because they were also tentmakers (Acts 18:3).

This tells me they were ordinary working people, yet they had the call of God resting upon their lives.

Priscilla means "ancient birth," and according to scripture, elders of the land, or the aged, are to receive respect. This is quite a contrast from today's world where those advanced in years are often considered "spent" or worthless—and even more chilling—some, if they could, would even put senior citizens out of their misery with euthanasia.

If you read the book of Proverbs, however, you'll learn that in God's sight, the wisdom which comes through experience is invaluable.

THE POWER OF TWO

When I encourage you to work along side your husband in ministry, you may respond, "But you don't understand, the man I married is no Aquila!"

Take my advice. If you will treat him as though he *were*, you might be surprised how soon God will transform him into such a person.

The power of two is a biblical principle:

- *"Two are better than one because they have a good return for their labor"* (Ecclesiastes 4:9).
- The disciples were sent out two by two. Jesus *"summoned the twelve and began to send*

them out in pairs" (Mark 6:7).
- The Bible says one shall *"chase a thousand"* but two shall *"put ten thousand to flight"* (Deuteronomy 32:30).

While every individual, married or single, has their particular assignment in God's Kingdom, in most cases, a born again couple, dedicated to the Lord and serving Him with their whole hearts, can do much more than a singular individual who loves the Lord and ministers alone.

A multiplication of power and effectiveness takes place in a couple serving together.

10. ESTHER
– "FOR SUCH A TIME AS THIS"

What a life of purpose Esther lived.

Her place in history began when Queen Vashti refused to attend a banquet as requested by her husband, Ahasuerus, King of Persia and Media.

Vashti was immediately banished from the palace and the king announced a beauty contest to determine who would replace her as queen.

In one of the regions there was a young virgin named Esther. Her relative, Mordecai, was raising her since both of her parents had died. No one knew she was Jewish and that her Hebrew name was Hadassah.

Esther won the contest in her region and was escorted to the palace to begin her preparation to lie with the king.

Regardless of her outer beauty, Esther may have had to cope with less than perfection inside. You see, Esther and Mordecai were from the tribe of Benjamin. As we discussed in the previous chapter, each tribe in Israel had a distinct personality and character trait. Benjamin's was something fierce!

Benjamin was Rachel's youngest son and Joseph's younger brother. After Rachel died, Jacob, his father undoubtedly protected and coddled young Benjamin, because his tribe grew to be troublesome.

When they refused to punish the brutal rapists among them, the tribe was nearly wiped out. Later on, the proud King Saul was a Benjaminite, and members of the tribe continued to resist David's succession even after Saul and his sons were killed. These traits were what Esther and Mordecai had stamped in their DNA. They were not necessarily sweet, loving, virtuous, spiritual people by default.

In order to become what the Lord intended, they had to overcome these inherent weaknesses—just as you and I must discipline our lives and bring any negative traits from our background into subjection and obedience to Christ and His Word.

I must add however, that these same strong personality characteristics can become powerful instruments for good when they are surrendered to God. The apostle Paul was from the tribe of Benjamin, as was the long-suffering prophet, Jeremiah.

DYING TO SELF

Regardless of what your natural inclinations are, you cannot blindly say, "Well, I'm Irish and have red hair, so I have a temper. Or, "I'm German, so I am stubborn. Just accept me the way I am."

No. God says, "You must live *this* way!"—and He explains how in His Word.

As a free moral agent you can make your own choices. I've met people who claim to be born again and may even teach a Sunday School class or sing in the choir, yet they have not placed many areas of their lives under subjection to Christ. As a result, they are missing much of what the Lord desires to accomplish in them. And inevitably, others suffer from their failure to obey God.

How do we change? We must die to self. This is a transformation which only comes from God—since we cannot crucify ourselves. I once heard someone say, "You might be able to tie your feet and drive a spike into one hand, but it would be impossible to do the same to the other hand." Self crucifixion is impossible.

It takes other people to accomplish it. And unfortunately, many are only too ready to try! The problem is, as soon as they start, we begin screaming, fighting, blaming them, and trying to find a way out.

But Jesus tells us, *"...unless a grain of wheat falls into the earth and dies, it remains alone; but if it dies, it bears much fruit"* (John 12:24).

We must be willing to let go of our rights, privileges and personality to everything we want, or feel we deserve. Only then can God bring new life in a dimension we never before thought possible.

TOTAL SUBMISSION

Everything about Jesus' trial and sentence was wrong, and actually illegal. Yet He humbly submitted, saying, *"Father, if You are willing, remove this cup from Me; yet not My will, but Yours be done"* (Luke 22:42).

It looked like the end. And so it is with us.

At some time in our life, we will be faced with the decision, "Is it going to be my way or God's way?" At that moment, choosing God's way may look like the end. Like Esther, we must decide, "If I never draw another happy breath, I am going to obey what God says!"

But remember, Satan had no idea of the plan behind the crucifixion. He didn't know there was a resurrection day coming. If we choose God's way, and wait on Him, He is more than able to bring forth a "resurrection" and reveal a plan no one ever suspected.

PLEASING THE KING

I believe Esther faced the same problems as you and I do today. Remember, she chose to be obedient to her earthly authority, Mordecai. And he was probably just as demanding as any Benjamite—not soft, gentle and kind.

Once inside the palace, Esther chose to be obedient to the authority of Hegai, the keeper of the kings harem. She found favor with him and *"...he quickly provided her with her cosmetics and food, gave her seven choice maids from the king's palace and transferred her and her maids to the best place in the harem"* (Esther 2:9).

Why? Because he knew the kings preference—what he liked.

There were probably 50 other women soaking in scented oils, learning every feminine enhancement and developing their seductive skills. It was a 12-month beautification and preparation program—getting ready to please King Ahasuerus.

All this for a king who certainly had his flaws. Read the account and you will soon learn he had a volatile temper—that's why he banished Queen Vashti from the palace. And once, according to Greek history, after a bridge had been built in the Persian empire, it buckled and collapsed in a storm. The king was so enraged he took a whip and actually scourged the sea because the bridge fell into the waters! And of course he executed the engineers who had built it.

This is the man Esther had to please.

WOULD SHE PERISH?

While Esther was living inside the palace, Mordecai hung around the gate, waiting for any morsel of news regarding her. In the meantime, an aide to the royal throne, Haman, was promoted, and an order went out that every person was to bow and pay homage to him.

Mordecai refused because it was God's law not to bow to any man, Then, when Haman discovered he was Jewish, angry, he determined to destroy not just Mordecai, but the entire Jewish race along with him—and coerced the king to make such a decree to the nation.

Esther heard that Mordecai was weeping before the palace gate, covered in sackcloth and ashes. She sent a trusted messenger to find out why—and Mordecai gave him the text of the decree for Esther to see for herself.

The time had come for her to plead for the lives of her people—yet the king still had no idea she was Jewish. Furthermore, she had not been called for recently, and no one was allowed to approach the king unless he first extended his royal scepter to them.

It was a horrendous situation to be in. The New American Standard translation says, "the queen writhed in great anguish" when her maidens and eunuchs came and told her what was going on.

She found courage in the words of Mordecai, who wrote in a note, "You may not want to do this, and perhaps God will bring deliverance from some other place. But if you remain silent, don't think you will escape any more than the rest of us." Then he added, *"...and who knoweth whether thou art come to the kingdom for such a time as this?"* (Esther 4.14 KJV).

Aware she was laying her life on the line by going to the king without an invitation, Esther chose to do what was required, saying, *"..if I perish, I perish"* (v.16).

"What is Troubling You?"

Esther and her maidens fasted and prayed for three days, while outside Mordecai and the Jews did the same. Then, *"Esther put on her royal robes and stood in the inner court of the king's palace in front of the king's rooms, and the king was sitting on his royal throne in the throne room, opposite the entrance to the palace. When the king saw Esther the queen standing in the court, she obtained favor in his sight; and the king extended to Esther the golden scepter which was in his hand. So Esther came near and touched the top of the scepter"* (Esther 5:1-2).

The king then asked, *"What is troubling you, Queen Esther? And what is your request? Even to half of the kingdom it shall be given to you"* (v.3).

Esther responded with great wisdom and tact, and God enabled the situation to be revealed at the right moment. The king ordered the treacherous Haman to be hanged, the Jews were spared, and Mordecai was promoted to a high position.

Think of it! The young girl became a beloved queen, and her uncle the prime minister—literally the heart and brains of the palace—because she trusted God and obeyed in an impossible situation.

However desperate your circumstance, or no matter how hopeless it may seem, remember the Lord has placed you here for a reason. Your Heavenly Father has a divine plan for your future.

TEN DIFFERENT WOMEN

These are only ten examples of the many women we find in the Bible. All of them are wonderful role models, from whom we can learn.

You may feel called to minister like one of them specifically, or perhaps a little bit of each of them at different times, as necessary. One thing is certain: As you seek Him with your whole heart, He will direct your steps, and cause you to become the woman He wants you to be.

1. Miriam—knowing bitterness, and leading others into worship.
2. Huldah—strong yet graceful, courageously speaking God's Word.
3. Deborah—a respected prophetess in high position.
4. Anna—the bright and happy intercessor in prayer.
5. Mary—she also knew bitterness, yet exemplified obedience.
6. Lydia—a competent businesswoman who prevailed.

7. Dorcas (or Tabitha)—creatively talented and resurrected.
8. Phoebe—the church deacon shining brightly for Him.
9. Priscilla—ministering along with her husband
10. Esther—placed in a critical position "for such a time as this."

CHAPTER 5

*S*ILENT NO MORE!

*I*t's remarkable how far women have advanced in just the past few decades. The "glass ceiling" has been shattered in many areas and women are now lauded judges, lawyers, CEO's of major corporations and prime ministers of nations. Yes, "You've come a long way, baby!"

But what about the church? The role of women in ministry is still a big question mark in many denominations—with some outright banning any female from ordination.

What does the Bible say regarding the matter of women in ministry? And how will you respond if the Lord places a special calling on your life?

THE "NO NO" VERSES

Let's jump right into the Bible passages which have caused controversy for generations. They have been called the "No No" verses. Paul writes to the church at Corinth, *"The women are to keep silent in the churches; for they are not permitted to speak, but are to subject themselves, just as the Law also says. If they desire to learn anything, let them ask their own husbands at home; for it is improper for a woman to speak in church"* (1 Corinthians 14:34-35).

For many, this is an open and shut case against women preachers. But wait a minute! These words have nothing at all to do with women presenting God's Word. Paul was answering questions dealing with the matter of how tongues and prophecy are to be handled in the congregation—since there are excesses and extremes and people are sometimes out of order.

A MATTER OF SELF-DISCIPLINE

In the cultural setting of those days, men sat on one side of the church and women on the other. And when a wife didn't understand what was being said, she would often call out to her husband for the answer—and he could be seated quite a distance from her! So the apostle was attempting to restore order and reverence to the services.

Earlier, when Paul was discussing the fact that women should have a covering on their head in the sanctuary, he writes, *"But every woman who has her head uncovered while praying or prophesying disgraces her head"* (1 Corinthians 11:5). Yes, he was speaking concerning *"when you come together as a church"* (v.18).

If Paul was implying women shouldn't speak in the house of God, this would be quite a contradiction since by its very nature, prophesying is a public act. If a woman prays at home alone, who cares whether or not her hair is covered!

Regarding impulsive outbursts and questions which

97

disrupt a service, Paul says a woman is to, of her own free will, discipline herself.

"A Sound Mind"

The Greek verb for "speak" used in 1 Corinthians 14:35 is "sigao"—the same word Paul used when giving instructions regarding a message in tongues during a service. He counseled, *"...if there is no interpreter, he must keep silent in the church; and let him speak to himself and to God"* (v.28).

Sigao means "to voluntarily muzzle oneself."

In other words, you have a choice whether or not you speak in tongues or whether or not to interpret. You bring yourself under self-discipline. Remember, *"...the spirits of the prophets are subject to the prophets"* (v.32 KJV).

I've seen individuals in some churches make public spectacles of themselves, bringing no honor or glory to God.

The Lord is looking for those who use wisdom concerning these matters: *"For God hath not given us the spirit of fear; but of power, and of love, and of a sound mind"* (2 Timothy 1:7 KJV).

A Peaceable Spirit

Another scripture used by those who want to keep women from being used in ministry is when Paul, writing to Timothy, stated, *"A woman must quietly receive instruction with entire submissiveness. But I do not allow a woman to teach or exercise authority over a man, but to remain quiet"* (1 Timothy 2:11-12).

There are certain churches who take this verse so literally they only allow a woman to teach a Sunday School class of young boys as long as they have not reached puberty—not yet men.

This is not what the Bible is referring to. Here, the Greek word for *silence* is "hesuchias"—"a tranquil, peaceable spirit." It is a demeanor; a way of behaving with dignity and quietness. And it's a noun, not a verb.

The apostle is saying a woman should not function without this *hesuchias*. This is the same word used in the beginning of the chapter when he writes, *"I urge that entreaties and prayers, petitions and thanksgivings, be made on behalf of all men, for kings and all who are in authority, so that we may lead a tranquil and quiet life in all godliness and dignity"* (vv.1-2).

Paul is asking women to *learn* with "hesuchias." This is not forbidding them to participate in the church, rather he is offering guidelines for receiving instruction.

We are not to be domineering, loud or overbearing. There is nothing more obnoxious or distracting than a woman who plows forward like a Sherman tank!

The Bible says, *"It is better to live in a corner of a roof than in a house shared with a contentious woman"* (Proverbs 21:9).

Our place in the body of Christ must be one which exemplifies Paul's admonition to lead a *"tranquil and quiet life in all godliness and dignity."*

Equal, Yet in Divine Order

In God's eyes, women and men are absolutely equal and

He does not place one above the other. Scripture declares, *"There is neither Jew nor Greek, there is neither slave nor free man, there is neither male nor female; for you are all one in Christ Jesus. And if you belong to Christ, then you are Abraham's descendants, heirs according to promise"* (Galatians 3:28-29).

It's been said, "At the foot of the cross, the ground is perfectly level."

At the same time, God's word recognizes there are distinct *differences* between the sexes, and that's why functional roles and lines of authority have been established.

No one would deny that Jesus Christ is co-equal with God—that the Father and Son are one. Yet, as we read scripture, Jesus was always submissive to the will of the Father. In the Garden of Gethsemane He prayed, *"Father, if You are willing, remove this cup from Me; yet not My will, but Yours be done"* (Luke 22:42).

Jesus recognized divine order and authority.

FAITH-FILLED WOMEN

In the "Roll Call of Faith," found in Hebrews 11, great men of the Old Testament are listed—including Noah, Moses and David.

However, many overlook the fact women are part of this important group. *"By faith...Sarah herself received ability to conceive, even beyond the proper time of life, since she considered Him faithful who had promised"* (v.11). And, *"By faith Rahab...did not perish along with those who were disobedient, after she had welcomed the spies in peace"* (v.31).

God has a place of service for *every* believer.

THE FIVE-FOLD MINISTRY

Still, the role of women holding positions of church leadership continues to be a point of discussion and dissension in many circles. For example, in setting requirements for deacons, Paul states, *"Deacons...must be men of dignity, not double-tongued, or addicted to much wine or fond of sordid gain...*[and] *beyond reproach"* (1 Timothy 3:10). Then in the next verse, on the same topic, he counsels, *"Women must likewise be dignified, not malicious gossips, but temperate, faithful in all things"* (v.11).

Remember, Pheobe was a *"servant of the church"* (Romans 16:1). Servant being translated from the Greek *diakonon*, or "deacon."

In the "five-fold ministry," the Lord *"...gave some as apostles, and some as prophets, and some as evangelists, and some as pastors and teachers, for the equipping of the saints for the work of service, to the building up of the body of Christ"* (Ephesians 4:11-12).

Do these offices have a "For Men Only" sign on the door? If we study God's Word, the answer is a resounding "No." For example, the Lord didn't exclusively call just men to prophesy, He also included women.

WHO SHALL PROPHESY?

Immediately after the Holy Spirit was poured out in the Upper Room, Peter announced to an amazed crowd who had gathered on the streets of Jerusalem, *"...but this is what was spoken of through the prophet Joel: 'And it shall be in the last days,' God says, 'that I will pour forth of My spirit on all mankind; and your sons and your daughters shall*

101

prophesy, and your young men shall see visions, and your old men shall dream dreams; even on my bondslaves, both men and women, I will in those days pour forth of my spirit and they shall prophesy. And I will grant wonders in the sky above and signs on the earth below, blood, and fire, and vapor of smoke. The sun will be turned into darkness and the moon into blood, before the great and glorious day of the Lord shall come. And it shall be that everyone who calls on the name of the Lord will be saved" (Acts 2:15-21).

Hallelujah! This prophecy is being fulfilled.

"Whosoever Will"

I thank God for the legacy of women evangelists, pastors and teachers such as Aimee Semple McPherson, Corrie Ten Boom and Kathryn Kuhlman who answered the call of the Lord and received an anointing from the Holy Spirit to touch millions of lives.

At the end of this chapter, I have included a list of women who are having an impact on today's generation.

God's invitation goes out to *"whosever will"* (Mark 8:34).

The Great Commission is for all—young and old, men and women. Jesus said, *"Go into all the world and preach the gospel to all creation. He who has believed and has been baptized shall be saved; but he who has disbelieved shall be condemned"* (Mark 16:15-16).

Then the Lord declares, *"These signs will accompany those who have believed."* (v.17). Only the men who have believed? No, it is all inclusive.

And here is what will happen in the ministry of these men and women: *"...in My name they will cast out demons, they will speak with new tongues; they will pick up serpents, and if they drink any deadly poison, it will not hurt them; they will lay hands on the sick, and they will recover"* (vv.17-18).

Women, rejoice! You have been commissioned to a ministry of preaching, of deliverance and of healing.

THE MINISTRY OF WOMEN CONTINUES

I'm thankful for the many wonderful women of our own generation who are ministering in so many different ways. Some work alongside their husbands, helping fulfill their visions and increasing the effectiveness of their ministries. Some have unique ministries alone.

I believe God has raised all of them up to help spread the Gospel to a population explosion on planet earth in these last days. If you don't like the particular cultural style or ministry of some of them, that's okay. There are other people who do, and will receive from it. Those individuals might be turned off by the ones you prefer.

In today's world, God is using a tremendous variety of women to glorify His Son—He offers something for everyone. Each one of them is making a significant contribution to the church and even to the world.

Here are just a few I happen to know about (in alphabetical order.) God bless them all, including those I inadvertently missed and the countless ones I don't know!

*M*other Angelica, Kay Arthur, Sharron Bailey, Julie Baker, Lori Bakker, Sandy Barnard, Jeri Barricks, Lisa Bevere, Darlene Bishop, Sarah Boland, Debbie Boone, Shirley Boone, Fortune Brayfield, Billye Brim, Kelli

Brinson, Fran Brown, Mary Brown, Joanne Bunce, Sandi Burris, Laura Bush, Juanita Bynum.

Shirley Caesar, Mary Colbert, Gloria Copeland, Jan Crouch, Laurie Crouch, Darelene Czech, Jackie Davis, Molly DeAndrea (recently deceased), Sue Dodge, Taffy Dollar, Sharon Dougherty, Ann Downing, Elizabeth Elliot, Gloria Elliot, Myrna Etheridge.

Catie Frates, Gloria Gaither, Leona Glenn, Vestal Goodman (recently deceased), Ruth Graham, Diana Hagee, Jane Hansen, Nancy Harmon, Susan Henshaw, Marilyn Hickey, Angie Connor-Hicks, Beverly Hils, Sharon Hoffman, Toedy Holley, Valerie Holmes, Frances Hunter.

Carla Ives, Cindy Jacobs, Judy Jacobs, Jeanne Johnson, Holley Joiner, Marble Joiner, Cheryl Kartsonakis, Carol Kornacki, Jill Kelly, Delia Knox, Beverly LaHaye, Nora Lam (recently deceased), Joanie Lamb, Debbie Lanier, Freda Lindsay, Anne Graham Lotz.

Patti MacLeod, Babbie Mason, Berniece Matejeck, Candy McKeithen, Carol McSpadden, Kate McVeigh, Alverna Messick, Tammy Faye Messner, Joyce Meyer, Monica Miles, Betty Mills, Beth Moore, Darlene Neptune, Marilyn Neubauer, Julie Nolan.

Stormy Omartian, Jan Painter, Karen Patton, Juliea Peace, Betty Ruth Price, Dottie Rambo, Lori Ray, Brenda Rifkogel, Arthelene Rippy, Aimee Reid-Sych (named after Aimee McPherson), Evelyn Roberts (recently deceased), Lindsay Roberts, Betty Jean Robinson, Betty Robison.

Cheryl Salem, Gwen Shaw, Dottie Snow, Shira Sorko-Ram, Dorothy Spaulding, Donna Spearman, Nancy Starkweather, Pam Stenzel, Pamela Stone, Luci Swindoll, Joni Erickson Tada, Mother Teresa (deceased), Pam

Thumb, Brenda Timberlake, Betty Tipton, Iverna Tompkins, Rebecca Park Totilo, Edith Tripp.

Jean Vanderclock, Rexella Van Impe, Melanie Walker, Sheila Walsh, Merla Watson, Kristi Watts, Cindy Way, Krista Weygand, Karen Wheaton, Paula White, Cathy Williams, Gayle Wolff.

AND EVEN MORE –

But not all ministry is carried out in the traditional sense. Women faithfully serve the kingdom of God in a myriad of other capacities, in homes, churches, ministries, music and businesses, both religious and secular. In some cases they serve prominently, and in others quietly behind the scenes. Here are just a few I know of, and I salute them all! Someday they will hear, "Well done, thou good and faithful servant …":

Cookie Aikin, Marti Araki, Ruth Ann Ayre, Rosemary Barnes, Diane Bish, Jan Bishop, Mary Ellen Bogard, Wiry Brantley, Edna Brooks, Christa Bunner, Janice Burnette, Jennifer Campbell, Charlene Carlisle, Annette Carnes, Peggy Carter, Jenny Chancey, Jennifer Chaney, Judy Church, Victoria Clark, Kristin Clements, Beth Cloud, Galena R. Conatser, Robin Cox, Harriet Craig, Jeannie Crowell, Jessica Curtis.

Ruth Ann Daly, Viola Davis, Becky Day, Jocelyn Dooley, Mildred Dortch, Lynn Doxie, Janice Evans, Peggy Fears, Franciska Fenderson, Jill Foster, Loice Funderburg, Debbie Futrell, Chris Gabriel, Barbara Gailey, Lynn Gibbons, Charlotte Gladden, Denise Glenn, Amy Grant, Cris Groendyke.

Abby Hargrave, Francene Hash, Caroline Hill, Gail Hill, Linda Hollies, Connie Hopper, Deborah Hurd, Mary Hutchison, Deborah Hutson, Dee Jakel, Lisa James, Barbara Johnson, Linda Kinde, Donna Knuth, Laura Kymla, Sharon Lichtman, Ginger Lindsay, Michelle Loyd.

Phyllis McClellan, Lori McCraw, Linda McLain, Jean McMurray, Terri Meeuwson, Veronica Messick, Diana Milburn, Carolyn Miles, Luvinia Miles, Monica Miles, Brenda Morse, Pam Muir, Rosalie Nagich, Janice Norwood, Cyndy Osborne, Janet Paschcal, Jamie Partlow, Carolyn Patterson, Sandy Patti, Martha Peace, Amanda Prather, Ronda Price.

Phyllis Robinson, Lisa Ryan, Maureen Salaman, Mary Scholten, Jean Schroder, Lucy Seay, Darla Sensabaugh, Dee Simmons, DeAndre Simmons-Manges, Ernestine Smith, Vanessa Smith, Nancy Smolak, Connie Socier, Janie Sperry, Cynthia Steele, Barbara Stevenson, Ann Stein, Cynthia Stewart, Rebecca St. James, LaDonna Taylor, Julie Tomkus, Tammy Trent, Joan Trim, Kathy Troccoli.

Penny Vandergraph, Kim VanderMolen, Florence Varbedian, Patricia Vawser, Barbara Vroman, Stephanie Walther, Elana Watson, Kristi Watts, Gayla Welch, Lisa Welch, Traca Williams, CeCe Winans, Vicki Winans, Linda Wolber, Sheryl Wright, Vicki Yohe, Terrance Zepke.

CHAPTER 6

*Y*OUR SPECIAL GIFT

I marvel at the sovereignty of God. The Bible says we have been *"...predestined according to His purpose who works all things after the counsel of His will"* (Ephesians 1:11).

I have always felt uncomfortable when people ask me about my background, because what I am involved in today is not because of education, career planning, or personal goals and ambitions. Without question, I believe God planned my life and knew in advance Garth and I should be together for the work with which we have been entrusted.

Why? Because the Lord had a mission *He* wanted to see accomplished—and was searching for willing vessels who would catch the vision

Please don't take this comment as disrespectful, but at times I feel we are almost like "puppets" in His hands. He gave each of us distinct gifts—unique personalities, abilities, purposes and aptitudes. But united together we are doing exactly what the Lord had planned long before we came on the scene.

It's not because we are exceptionally smart or talented. We were just two ignorant kids—who often demonstrated our lack of knowledge. But through the years God has fulfilled His purposes through us, just as He has done with people throughout every generation.

If Garth and I had failed to heed God's call, I sincerely feel the Lord would have raised up someone else. I remember hearing Kathryn Khulman say, "I believe there were three other people God spoke to who were supposed to do this particular ministry. They said 'No'—so the Lord called me. And here I am."

We may not always be able to see where God is taking us, yet if we are faithful in the small tasks, day by day, He will lead us to the place He has destined.

GIFTS OF THE SPIRIT

Instinctively we all understand what a "gift" is— something we receive without earning it, simply offered by the good will of another. The Bible says much about gifts. Those who study it understand the most profound, and yet most simple gift of all: salvation is a gift of God, received by faith, not by working for it.

Beyond that, there are several other passages concerning "gifts" in the church and, quite honestly, we sometimes have a hard time putting it all together, and get bogged down in the details. Then, we start arguing about them with our brothers and sisters in Christ, and get into heated discussions over how many angels can dance on the head of a pin.

So before going any further, without getting into great detail, I'd like to share one foundational understanding with you.

In the New Testament there are three major passages about gifts. They reveal that each member of the Godhead has given His own particular gifts to the church.

First: Romans 12 tells us about the gifts of the *Father*, often called "Motivational Gifts." They are aptitudes, abilities and talents God has placed within you. It's how He created you to be, not what you decide to become. (They are what you just naturally do without even thinking. Each one has strengths *and* weaknesses—but that's another study.)

Second: 1 Corinthians 14 tells about the gifts of the *Spirit,* which are actually manifestations of the Holy Spirit, not us, working in different ways. (What a grand time we have arguing over these!)

Third: Ephesians 4 tells us about the gifts of the *Son,* which are five specific ministry offices that He calls individuals to fill—Apostle, Prophet, Evangelist, Pastor, Teacher. (Countless books are written concerning what those are—and aren't!)

In this chapter I want to show you the contrast between the "Gifts of the Spirit" and the "Motivation Gifts" presented in Romans." As a woman, I believe this will help you understand what the Lord desires to do through your life.

Let's begin with the "Gifts of the Spirit."

Paul declares, *"...there are varieties of gifts, but the same Spirit. And there are varieties of ministries, and the same Lord. There are varieties of effects, but the same God who works all things in all persons"* (1 Corinthians 12:4-6).

He then explains how the Holy Spirit gives individuals separate abilities *"for the common good"* (v.7).

The nine gifts listed are:

1. The word of wisdom (v.8).
2. The word of knowledge (v.8).
3. Faith (v.9).
4. Healing (v.9).
5. Miracle-working (v.10).
6. Prophecy (v.10).
7. Discerning of spirits (v.10).
8. Tongues (v.10).
9. The interpretation of tongues (v.10).

Once more we are reminded, *"But one and the same Spirit works all these things, distributing to each one individually just as He wills"* (v.11).

HIS ACTS, HIS ABILITIES

Please understand, these gifts of the Spirit are a manifestation of the *Holy Spirit*—of His acts and His abilities at separate times according to the need.

We cannot "work these up" within ourselves. They are given to the body of Christ at moments when *He* deems necessary.

For example, the word of wisdom is a supernatural understanding of a given situation—an inner guidance and direction to know exactly what to do.

The gift of the word of knowledge allows God to reveal an instantaneous insight of an event or circumstance you would never know in the natural.

You receive the gift of faith at a specific time for a specific purpose. The presence of the Holy Spirit descends because faith is necessary for miraculous things to happen. The Bible says each of us has a small measure of the gift of faith, but it is multiplied when the Spirit arrives on the scene.

Gifts of healings and miracles function through believers which produce awesome manifestations of God's mighty power.

The gift of prophecy is given for edification and comfort—because the Lord desires to redeem the situation or change it for the better.

THE EVIDENCE!

There is also the gift of discerning of spirits. The Holy Spirit will reveal to you when it is not just flesh and blood you are dealing with, but demons who need to be confronted. You don't argue or counsel—in the name of

Jesus you cast them out! And they will flee.

The gift of tongues and the interpretation of tongues did not cease with the apostles. Jesus included tongues when He said, *"These signs will accompany those who have believed"* (Mark 16:17). Literally millions of people living today have personally experienced this glorious evidence of the Holy Spirit.

His Glory, Not Ours

Believers who function in these special areas don't go around bragging, "I have the gift of discernment"—or wisdom, etc. No, the Holy Spirit *"works all these things, distributing to each one individually just as He wills"* (1 Corinthians 12:11). It is His decision when these manifestations occur.

God graciously gives these gifts as needed as we walk in obedience to Him. They operate in the body of Christ where the Holy Spirit is glorified and allowed the freedom to operate.

Motivation Gifts

As we discussed, these are not the only spiritual gifts mentioned in scripture. Paul, writing to the believers in Rome, presents a distinct list.

The reason these have been called the "Motivation Gifts," is because they are what lights your fire, what directs you inwardly and what spurs you to great accomplishments for the Lord. And, as we will see, they operate uniquely in each individual.

Paul says, *"Since we have gifts that differ according to the grace given to us, each of us is to exercise them accordingly "* (Romans 12:6).

The specific gifts he mentions include:

- Prophesy (v.6).
- Service (v.7).
- Teaching (v.7).
- Exhortation (v.8).
- Giving (v.8).
- Leadership (v.8).
- The showing of mercy (v.8).

If the Lord has generously entrusted you with one of these gifts, you will know it because you will have a natural inclination in this area—whether it is leadership, service or teaching. And people should not force you to become something God didn't intend for you to be.

It is human nature to criticize one another and often we have a tendency to think everyone should have the same gifts as ourselves. But that's not how God's will is accomplished.

THE VISIONARY

Perhaps you have noticed that "prophecy" appears in both the Gifts of the Spirit and the Motivation Gifts. But they are separate in nature. Prophesying in First Corinthians refers to seeing future events. However, a person with a prophetic *motive* (as in Romans 12) is a visionary regarding practical matters—knowing what needs to be done and speaking clearly to a situation.

The Bible states, *"Where there is no vision, the people perish"* (Proverbs 29:18 KJV). If there is no drive, no one to pull things together and give direction, the dream will die.

Two Different Gifts

My husband, Garth, clearly has a prophetic motivational gift and mine is one of mercy. As I jokingly told him recently, "If I didn't have mercy, I sure wouldn't put up with some of the things you do!"

But in truth, if Garth did not have the prophetic motivation which envisions, organizes, administers and speaks, he wouldn't be able to tolerate some of the things I do!

When there is a strong leader, people around such an individual must yield to his vision and authority.

Strengths and Weaknesses

In marriage, each person needs to recognize and respect the gifts in the other. When two distinct personalities join together it's almost like putting two cats in a bag and letting them fight it out!

But if you're smart, you will realize that each partner has strengths and weaknesses in their style and approach. In our case, Garth is strong and wise while I am the peacemaker, attempting to apply mercy to every situation.

God places two people together with varied gifts and each will make up for the deficiencies of the other.

They say opposites attract, and there's a good reason for it. Combined, we make the whole—more powerful and effective than either of us individually.

"I Was Made For This!"

Look carefully at each of these motivation gifts. Which one do you believe the Lord has called you to operate in?

You will know which is your calling because it is your natural tendency, what you delight in doing—what you perform automatically without even thinking about it.

Certain individuals claim a clear call to "service"—or "ministry." It feels a perfect fit for them and they have a built-in aptitude to serve others. In whatever capacity you see them, they are always helping and assisting.

You'll hear them say, "I was made for this!"

A person with a "teaching" motivation gift knows the Lord has given them an inner drive to impart knowledge to others. They have a God-given ability to teach.

However, if you try to ask a person with a "teaching"

motivation to pick up after others or be a servant, you'll immediately sense a hesitation, a resistance.

Others have the gift of "exhortation." Born speakers, who through their well-chosen words, encourage others to improve and succeed.

These verbal communicators are exciting to be around.

The Generous Giver

Thank God for those with the gift of "giving." Garth and I have met men and women who have donated large sums of money to various ministries. I believe the Lord allows these individuals to enjoy financial abundance because they have demonstrated faithfulness and trust.

Some people exclaim, "Oh, if I could just win the lottery, I would be able to give so much to God's work."

I doubt it! If an individual is not a natural giver when they have little in their hands, they will not suddenly be generous when they have plenty.

Next, some are blessed with a "leadership" motivation gift—often called "guiding" or "ruling." It's similar to a prophetic visionary, but here the focus is on strong administrative ability.

The final motivation gift listed in this passage is "mercy." It's the one that operates in me personally.

The individual who demonstrates compassion is to present it *"with cheerfulness"* (Romans 12:8).

A Unique View

You may have small portions of several of these motivation gifts, but most likely there is one which will stand head and shoulders above the rest. It is primary to your existence and the gift God desires just for you.

Looking at life through the prism of your special gift will cause you to have a unique view of the world—yet it is the picture you are supposed to have.

As any traffic accident investigator will tell you, two people witnessing the same car wreck will describe it totally different.

I like the example I once heard of what happens when a person drops a vase on the floor and it shatters all over the place. There is broken glass, crushed flowers and water running everywhere.

Several people are present and they each have a different response to the event:

- The person with the "prophetic" gift will say disapprovingly, "You should have held on tighter." (Intending to help the offender do better in the future.)
- The one with the "mercy" gift will comment kindly, "That's all right honey, we've all dropped something occasionally. Don't worry about it." (Wanting to help relieve the offenders embarrassment.)

- The individual with a "service" gift, will run and grab a mop, a dustpan and immediately clean up the mess. (Happy as can be to be doing something useful.)
- The person with the "teaching" gift will instruct, "Now the correct thing to do in this situation is to hold the glass with your fingers around it and have one hand supporting underneath...etc., etc..."
- The "exhorter" will say, "I know you meant to hold it right, but if you pay a little more attention it won't happen again. It's not hard and I know you can to it...blah, blah, blah..."
- The one with a gift of "giving" will open her purse and offer, "Here's some money. Go and buy a new vase." (Feeling greatly satisfied to have provided financially.)
- The individual with a "leadership" or administrative gift will immediately jump into action and direct the operation, pointing to different people: "You get the dust pan. You get the mop. You go get some more flowers. You find another vase." (Instinctively sensing that some supervision is needed here!)

These responses are each offering legitimate perspectives, and all should be welcome. Though different, none are wrong—all provide something necessary.

GOD'S "PRESENT" FOR YOU

Today, if for some reason you are not one hundred percent certain of your God-given gift, spend as much time with the Lord as it takes until He makes His will and your purpose clear.

When that moment arrives, praise Him for the wonderful "present" He has given you. It will be a great and rewarding gift for your life!

CHAPTER 7

*T*IME FOR A CHANGE

*M*ore than once, I've met women who say, "Tina, please pray for my husband. If he would just change, everything would be okay!"

After a few minutes of conversation, however, I realize that before the husband can be changed, there needs to be a major transformation in *her!*

The prayer the Lord is waiting to hear is "Lord, change me!"

With a contrite heart, ask your Heavenly Father, "Reveal to me what is displeasing to You and show me what I can do to bring peace and harmony to our home."

Only when you become a yielded vessel, willing to be reshaped and molded by the Potter's hand, will you begin to see the spiritual awakening in your husband for which you are praying.

Breaking Barriers

It's been said, "Marriage is all about forgiveness"—and it's true. Spouses often wound each other terribly, even though it's often unintentional. For example, a wife may simply be trying to make her husband see and feel what she is personally experiencing—and longing for her mate to accept what is important to her.

Unfortunately, in these pressure situations the battle between the sexes is often intensified.

How can the barriers of past mistakes be broken? Only when at least one of the partners totally submits to the Lord and chooses the path of forgiveness.

Read what Jesus said to the woman who was accused of adultery by the scribes and Pharisees. As they were about to stone her according to religious law, they asked Him, What would you do?"

The Lord's answer surprised them. He looked at these so-called righteous men and said, *"He who is without sin among you, let him be the first to throw a stone at her"* (John 8:7).

One by one, these guilty men vanished from the scene. Then Jesus looked at the woman and asked, *"Where are they? Did no one condemn you?"* (v.10).

"No one, Lord," she answered.

Forgiving her, Jesus said, *"I do not condemn you, either. Go. From now on sin no more"* (v.11).

The Forgiveness Factor

Of course there will be times the actions of a husband or wife will cause a deep, emotional wound. But should we respond by retaliating and seeking revenge, hurting the person in return? Or, should we try the "silent treatment," pulling away and isolating ourselves from any communication?

According to God's Word we are to demonstrate forgiveness. *"Be kind to one another, tender-hearted, forgiving each other, just as God in Christ also has forgiven you"* (Ephesians 4:32).

Peter once asked the Lord how many times he should forgive someone who sinned against him. Probably thinking he was being quite magnanimous, he said, "Up to seven times?" (Matthew 18:21).

Jesus answered, *"I do not say to you, up to seven times, but up to seventy times seven"* (Matthew 18:21-22).

To be on the receiving end of Christ's forgiveness, we must be willing to forgive.

The Road of Humility

You may be able to quote scripture from Genesis to Revelation, and feel that because you attend church, pay your tithe and are a prayer warrior, the Lord has an obligation to save your husband.

In the process of trying to be God-centered, some

women become *self*-centered.

Perhaps they need to ask themselves this question, "Am I so filled with spiritual pride that I am hindering the Lord from working in my home?"

The Bible tells us, *"Do nothing from selfishness or empty conceit, but with humility of mind regard one another as more important than yourselves; do not merely look out for your own personal interests, but also for the interests of others"* (Philippians 2:3-4).

I'm sure the Lord won't mind if you start spending more time with your husband!

SET YOUR SAILS!

The life-altering experience God is looking for starts on the inside. Yes, the Lord wants to cleanse our heart, but He also desires to change our thoughts.

Scripture tells us, *"And do not be conformed to this world, but be transformed by the renewing of your mind, so that you may prove what the will of God is, that which is good and acceptable and perfect"* (Romans 12:2).

Your thoughts are like the sails of a ship. Where they lead you depends on how you set them. In the words of a poem by an unknown author:

> *One ship goes East another West*
> *By the selfsame winds that blow*
> *'Tis the set of the sail and not the gale*
> *That determines the way they go.*

Like the ships at sea are the ways of fate
As we journey along through life
'Tis the set of the soul that decides the goal
And not the calm or strife.

God's Word directs His children to *"Set your mind on the things above, not on the things that are on earth"* (Colossians 3:2).

Only He can truly calm the storms of life and lead you to a safe harbor.

It's Your Call!

Whether you choose God's way or your own independent path is your personal decision—but please realize your final destination is at stake.

Joshua said to the rebellious children of Israel, many who were still serving false gods: *"...choose for yourselves today whom you will serve"* (Joshua 24:15). However, he made his own decision perfectly clear: *"...but as for me and my house, we will serve the Lord"* (v.15).

A "Living Epistle"

Read God's Word and allow inspired scripture to point out the choices you need to make in both your thoughts and behavior. As you pray and work on improving yourself, you will notice the situations around you will also be enhanced.

How is this possible? God is alive and working through you. Suddenly you are a living epistle, demonstrating the fruit of the Spirit—*"love, joy, peace, patience, kindness, goodness, faithfulness, gentleness, self-control"* (Galatians 5:22-23).

As a woman who has been chosen and beloved by the Lord, you are to have *"...a heart of compassion, kindness, humility, gentleness and patience; bearing with one another, and forgiving each other, whoever has a complaint against anyone; just as the Lord forgave you, so also should you"* (Colossians 3:12-13).

What a drastic impact these qualities will make—both in you and those you love.

LET CHRIST RULE

What wife or mother enjoys constant arguments and war in the home? We are told to discard conflict and *"...put on love, which is the perfect bond of unity"* (Colossians 3:14).

In a world of terror and turmoil, when it seems we have no control, make the choice to *"Let the peace of Christ rule in your hearts...Let the word of Christ richly dwell within you, with all wisdom [and] ...Whatever you do in word or deed, do all in the name of the Lord Jesus, giving thanks through Him to God the Father"* (vv.15-17).

GOD'S DESIRE

On these pages we have talked about love, respect, self, submission, and the godly characteristics which the Lord desires in a woman.

It is my prayer that as you put these principles into daily practice, God will bless and honor your relationships, strengthen your home and help you to become the person He has created you to be.

To Contact the Author
or to Learn More About TCT:

TCT Ministries
P.O. Box 1010
Marion, IL 62959

Phone: 618-997-9333
U.S. Prayer Center: 313-534-1818
Internet: www.tct.tv
Email: correspondence@tct.tv